Praise for *Lincoln's Greatest Speech*

"This is the very best book on the most famous of all inaugural addresses."

—Frank J. Williams, chairman of the Lincoln Forum

"Those who think it is not possible to say anything fresh about the life and convictions of Abraham Lincoln will be surprised by this book. Careful attention to the complex layers of Lincoln's own actions and beliefs leaves Ronald White with a rich harvest of religious, political, and social insight concerning what truly was Lincoln's Greatest Speech. "

—Mark A. Noll, author of *America's God: From Jonathan Edwards to Abraham Lincoln*

"Ronald C. White's elegantly written study of Lincoln's Second Inaugural offers a close examination of both the form and the substance of Lincoln's address."

—David Herbert Donald, author of *Lincoln*

"Delightful . . . without question our best commentary on Lincoln's deepest and most intellectually self-revealing speech."

—Allen C. Guelzo, *The Christian Century*

"White is very good on Lincoln's rhetorical techniques. . . . He shows us how such rhetorical devices reveal character and create meaning. . . . He also has a good eye for vivid quotation."

—Max Byrd, *The New York Times Book Review*

"White presents his points with great erudition. . . . [He] fills the pages with delightful details, and brings this great speech into the light of modern analysis."

—Ed Malles, *The Orlando Sentinel*

"A masterful mix of history, biography, and rhetoric . . . wise yet humble in its judgments."

—David Reinhard, *The Oregonian*

"Does for Lincoln's Second Inaugural something of what Garry Wills did for the Gettysburg Address."

—*Publishers Weekly*

"A thoughtful historical, cultural, and literary meditation . . . Effectively illuminates the greatness of Lincoln's perceptive intellect and formidable character. Well researched, wonderfully written, and at times extraordinarily moving. . . . Comes closer to finding the true spirit of Abraham Lincoln than many of the more celebrated biographies."

—*Kirkus Reviews* (starred)

"A masterly explication of both the text and context of the speech . . . brings meaning to Lincoln's words."

—Gregory J. Sullivan, *First Things*

"September 11, 2001, told us that we need Lincoln more than ever. Ronald White's book with its high ideals is thoughtful, inspiring, and ingenious. A very good read for this time and all time. A rare treat!"

—Gabor S. Boritt, director of the Civil War Institute at Gettysburg College

ALSO BY RONALD C. WHITE JR.

The Social Gospel:
Religion and Reform in Changing America
(with C. Howard Hopkins)

American Christianity:
A Case Approach
(with Garth Rosell and Louis B. Weeks)

Partners in Peace and Education
(Editor with Eugene J. Fisher)

Liberty and Justice for All:
Racial Reform and the Social Gospel

An Unsettled Arena:
Religion and the Bill of Rights
(Editor with Albright G. Zimmerman)

LINCOLN'S GREATEST SPEECH

The Second Inaugural

Ronald C. White Jr.

SIMON & SCHUSTER PAPERBACKS

NEW YORK   LONDON   TORONTO   SYDNEY

For
The Huntington Library,
Art Collections, and Botanical Gardens—
A Home away from Home

SIMON & SCHUSTER PAPERBACKS
Rockefeller Center
1230 Avenue of the Americas
New York, NY 10020

This Simon & Schuster trade paperback edition 2006
SIMON & SCHUSTER PAPERBACKS and colophon are registered trademarks
of Simon & Schuster, Inc.

For information about special discounts for bulk purchases,
please contact Simon & Schuster Special Sales:
1-800-456-6798 or business@simonandschuster.com.

Designed by Katy Riegel
Manufactured in the United States of America

1   3   5   7   9   10   8   6   4   2

The Library of Congress has cataloged the
Simon & Schuster hardcover edition as follows:
White, Ronald C. (Cedric), date.
Lincoln's greatest speech : the second inaugural / Ronald C. White Jr.
p. cm.
Includes bibliographical references and indexes.
1. Lincoln, Abraham, 1809–1865—Inauguration, 1865.
2. Lincoln, Abraham, 1809–1865—Oratory. 3. Lincoln, Abraham,
1809–1865—Literary art. 4. Presidents—United States—Inaugural addresses.
5. Speeches, addresses, etc., American—History and criticism. I. Title.

E457.94 1865d
973.7'092—dc21   2001054234

ISBN-13: 978-0-7432-1298-4
ISBN-10:   0-7432-1298-3
ISBN-13: 978-0-7432-9962-6 (Pbk)
ISBN-10:   0-7432-9962-0 (Pbk)

"The address sounded more like a sermon than a state paper."

— Frederick Douglass,
March 4, 1865

CONTENTS

LINCOLN'S GREATEST SPEECH

Fellow Countrymen:

At this second appearing to take the oath of the presidential office, there is less occasion for an extended address than there was at the first. Then a statement, somewhat in detail, of a course to be pursued, seemed fitting and proper. Now, at the expiration of four years, during which public declarations have been constantly called forth on every point and phase of the great contest which still absorbs the attention, and engrosses the energies of the nation, little that is new could be presented. The progress of our arms, upon which all else chiefly depends, is as well known to the public as to myself; and it is, I trust, reasonably satisfactory and encouraging to all. With high hope for the future, no prediction in regard to it is ventured.

On the occasion corresponding to this four years ago, all thoughts were anxiously directed to an impending civil war. All dreaded it—all sought to avert it. While the inaugeral address was being delivered from this place, devoted altogether to saving the Union without war, insurgent agents were in

the city seeking to destroy it without war-seek-
ing to dissolve the Union, and divide effects, by negotiation. Both parties deprecated war; but one
of them would make war rather than let the
nation survive; and the other would accept
war rather than let it perish. And the war
came.

One eighth of the whole
population were colored slaves, not distributed generally over the Union, but localized
in the Southern part half of it. These slaves constituted a peculiar and powerful interest.
All knew that this interest was, somehow,
the cause of the war. To strengthen, perpetuate, and extend this interest was the object for which the insurgents would rend
the Union, even by war; while the government claimed no right to do more than
to restrict the territorial enlargement of it.
Neither party expected for the war, the magnitude, or the duration, which it has already
attained. Neither anticipated that

the cause of the conflict might cease with, or even before, the conflict itself should cease. Each looked for an easier triumph, and a result less fundamental and astounding. Both read the same Bible, and pray to the same God; and each invokes His aid against the other. It may seem strange that any men should dare to ask a just God's assistence in wringing their bread from the sweat of other men's faces; but let us judge not that we be not judged. The prayers of both could not be answered; that of neither has been answered fully. The Almighty has His own purposes. "Woe unto the world because of offences! for it must needs be that offences come; but woe to that man by whom the offence cometh!" If we shall suppose that American Slavery is one of those offences which, in the providence of God, must needs come, but which, having continued through His appointed time, He now wills to remove, and that He gives to both North and South, this terrible war, as the woe due to those

by whom the offence came, shall we discern therein
in any departure from those divine attributes
which the believers in a living God always
ascribe to Him? Fondly do we hope— fervently do we pray— that this mighty scourge of
war may speedily pass away. Yet, if God
wills that it continue, until all the wealth
piled by the bond-man's two hundred and
fifty years of unrequited toil shall be sunk,
and until every drop of blood drawn with the
lash, shall be paid by another drawn with
the sword, as was said three thousand years
ago, so still it must be said "the judgments
of the Lord, are true and righteous altogether"
          With malice toward none;
with charity for all; with firmness in the
right, as God gives us to see the right,
let us strive on to finish the work we
are in; to bind up the nation's wounds;
to care for him who shall have borne the battle, and for his widow, and his orphan—
to do all which may achieve and cherish a just,
and a lasting peace, among ourselves, and with all nations.

Fellow Countrymen: [March 4, 1865]

At this second appearing, to take the oath of the presidential office, there is less occasion for an extended address than there was at the first. Then a statement, somewhat in detail, of a course to be pursued, seemed fitting and proper. Now, at the expiration of four years, during which public declarations have been constantly called forth on every point and phase of the great contest which still absorbs the attention, and engrosses the enerergies [sic] of the nation, little that is new could be presented. The progress of our arms, upon which all else chiefly depends, is as well known to the public as to myself; and it is, I trust, reasonably satisfactory and encouraging to all. With high hope for the future, no prediction in regard to it is ventured.

On the occasion corresponding to this four years ago, all thoughts were anxiously directed to an impending civil war. All dreaded it—all sought to avert it. While the inaugeral [sic] address was being delivered from this place, devoted altogether to *saving* the Union without war, insurgent agents were in the city seeking to *destroy* it without war—seeking to dissole [sic] the

Union, and divide effects, by negotiation. Both parties deprecated war; but one of them would *make* war rather than let the nation survive; and the other would *accept* war rather than let it perish. And the war came.

One eighth of the whole population were colored slaves, not distributed generally over the Union, but localized in the Southern part of it. These slaves constituted a peculiar and powerful interest. All knew that this interest was, somehow, the cause of the war. To strengthen, perpetuate, and extend this interest was the object for which the insurgents would rend the Union, even by war; while the government claimed no right to do more than to restrict the territorial enlargement of it. Neither party expected for the war, the magnitude, or the duration, which it has already attained. Neither anticipated that the *cause* of the conflict might cease with, or even before, the conflict itself should cease. Each looked for an easier triumph, and a result less fundamental and astounding. Both read the same Bible, and pray to the same God; and each invokes His aid against the other. It may seem strange that any men should dare to ask a just God's assistance in wringing their bread from the sweat of other men's faces; but let us judge not that we be not judged. The prayers of both could not be answered; that of neither has been answered fully. The Almighty has his own purposes. "Woe unto the world because of offences! for it must needs be that offences come; but woe to that man by whom the offence cometh!" If we shall suppose that American Slavery is one of those offences which, in the providence of God, must needs come, but which, having continued through His appointed time, He now wills to remove, and that He gives to both North and South, this terrible war, as the woe due to those by whom the offence came, shall we discern therein any departure from those divine attributes which the believers in a Living God always ascribe to Him? Fondly do we hope—fervently do we pray—that this mighty scourge of war may speedily pass away. Yet, if God wills that it continue, until all the wealth piled by the bond-man's two hundred and fifty years of unrequited toil shall be sunk, and until every drop of blood drawn with the lash, shall be paid by another drawn with the sword, as was said three thousand years ago, so still it must be said "the judgments of the Lord, are true and righteous altogether[."]

With malice toward none; with charity for all; with firmness in the right, as God gives us to see the right, let us strive on to finish the work we are in; to bind up the nation's wounds; to care for him who shall have borne the battle, and for his widow, and his orphan—to do all which may achieve and cher-ish a just, and a lasting peace, among ourselves, and with all nations.

1

Inauguration Day

President Abraham Lincoln had every reason to be hopeful as inauguration day, March 4, approached in 1865. The Confederacy was splintered, if not shattered. On February 1, Union General William Tecumseh Sherman led sixty thousand troops out of Savannah. Slashing through South Carolina, they wreaked havoc in the state that had been the seedbed of secession. To celebrate victories in Columbia and Charleston, South Carolina, and Wilmington, North Carolina, Lincoln ordered a nighttime illumination in Washington, on February 22, the birthday of George Washington. Crowds celebrated these achievements in song as the harbinger of the end of the hostilities.

At the same time, Union General Ulysses S. Grant was besieging Petersburg, Virginia, twenty miles south of Richmond. Despite Confederate General Robert E. Lee's previous record for forestalling defeat, it was clear that the badly outnumbered Confederates could not hold out much longer. Everything pointed toward victory.

Apprehension intruded upon this hopeful spirit. Rumors were flying about the capital that desperate Confederates, now realizing that defeat was imminent, would attempt to abduct or assassinate the president. Secretary of War Edwin

M. Stanton took extraordinary precautions. All roads leading to Washington had been heavily picketed for some days and the bridges patrolled with "extra vigilance." The 8th Illinois Cavalry was sent out from Fairfax Court House with orders to look for "suspicious characters." The problem was greatly complicated by the presence of large numbers of Confederate deserters who now roamed the capital. Stanton posted sharpshooters on the buildings that would ring the inaugural ceremonies. Plainclothes detectives roved the city keeping track of questionable persons.[1]

After four years as a war president, Lincoln could look ahead to four years as a peace president. With no Congress in session until December to hamper him, he would have free rein to do some peacemaking on his own.[2]

Gamblers were even betting that the sixteenth president would be inaugurated for a third term in 1869. The president, who had been battered by critics in Congress and the press for much of the war, was finally beginning to receive credit for his leadership. Many were suggesting that the stakes were about to get higher. Would Lincoln, the resourceful commander-in-chief in war, guide a reunited nation during what was beginning to be called "Reconstruction"?

———

As the day for his second inauguration drew near, everyone wondered what the president would say. No one seemed to know anything about the content of Lincoln's Second Inaugural Speech. A dispatch from the Associated Press reported that the address would be "brief—not exceeding, probably a column in length." It was recalled that he took thirty-five minutes to deliver his First Inaugural Address. The *New York Herald* reported, "The address will probably be the briefest one ever delivered." Another report said the address would take only five to eight minutes. There was great curiosity about the substance of this president's address.[3]

If reports about the length of the address were correct, how would Lincoln deal with questions that were multiplying? Would he use his rhetorical skills to "take the hide off" his opponents in the South and North? Was the Confederate States of America to be treated as a conquered nation? How did one demarcate between the innocent and the guilty, between citizens and soldiers? What would Lincoln say about the slaves? They had been emancipated, but what about the matter of suffrage?

All of these questions involved complex constitutional issues. Lincoln had used a good portion of his First Inaugural to argue carefully and logically his understanding of the indissoluble Union in light of the Constitution. The *New York World,* a newspaper in the city of New York that had been a thorn in his side all through the war, offered Lincoln advice. The correspondent contended that the Second Inaugural Address "ought to be the most significant and reassuring of all his public utterances."[4]

Just beneath the outward merry-making lay a different emotion. A weariness of spirit pervaded the nation. Government officials were fatigued from four long years of war. The agony of battle took its toll on families everywhere. Many citizens were filled with as much anger as hope. Even the anticipation of victory could not compensate for the loss of so many young men, cut down in death or disabled by horrible wounds just as they were preparing to harvest the fruits of their young lives.

And death and despair reached into nearly every home. The enormity of the human loss in the Civil War reaches us across time. An estimated 623,000 men died in the Civil War. One out of eleven men of service age was killed between

1861 and 1865. Comparisons with other wars bring it home. In World War I, the number killed was 117,000. In World War II, 405,000 died. In the Korean War, the death toll was 54,000. In the war in Vietnam, the number of Americans killed was 58,000. Deaths in the Civil War almost equal the number killed in all subsequent wars.

In three small towns in Massachusetts, people knew their young men by name and by family. New Braintree, with its total population of 805 shopkeepers, laborers, farmers, and their families, sent 78 young men to fight; 10 did not return. Phillipston, population 764, dispatched 76 of its young citizens to fight; 9 died on battlefields. The people of Auburn watched their 97 soldiers go off to war; they would mourn for each of the 15 who never returned.[5]

The people of the United States in the early 1860s felt the impact of war in their small communities. Had World War II produced the same proportion of deaths as did the Civil War, more than two and a half million men would have died. The loss of so many fathers, husbands, brothers, and sons usurped the joy and reward of imminent victory.

Washington had never seen so many people as those who converged on the capital for Lincoln's second inauguration. Trains roared and smoked over the double tracks of the Baltimore and Ohio. Delegations from north and west streamed through the freshly decorated B & O depot. The *Washington Daily National Intelligencer* reported, "Every train was crowded to repletion." Visitors were greeted by a band playing "The Battle Cry of Freedom." Each day the Washington newspapers listed the notables who were arriving. All knew they were coming to witness a unique event.[6]

Hotels were overflowing. Willard's, the grand five-story hotel at the corner of Pennsylvania Avenue and Fourteenth

Street, had cots in its halls and parlors. The Metropolitan and the National were filled. "The hotels are literally shelving their guests," reported the correspondent for the *New York Times*.[7] Lincoln-Johnson Clubs lodged more than a thousand visitors. Firehouses offered sleeping spaces.

For the first time, the idea had taken hold to make this inauguration a national holiday. Festivities were planned for Saturday, March 4, in New York, Boston, Chicago, St. Louis, San Francisco, and many smaller cities and towns. Banks and public offices would be closed. In Jersey City, there was to be a display of flags from public buildings, shipping, and private dwellings. St. Louis planned to conclude the day with an exhibition of fireworks. In New York City, church bells were to be rung for one half-hour in connection with the "national celebration and Union Victory." Churches announced special worship services on inauguration day. There would be prayers for the re-elected president.[8]

Vindication marched with victory in the early spring of 1865. Friends and supporters of the president, who was beleaguered during much of his first term, now declared that the recent events vindicated his leadership. The *Illinois Daily State Journal,* a friend of Lincoln's from his earliest campaigns as a legislator in Illinois, recalled his words in the First Inaugural and the results of the war. The March 4 editorial declared, "All honor to Abraham Lincoln through whose honesty, fidelity, and patriotism, those glorious results have been achieved."[9] The *Chicago Tribune,* also a staunch supporter, stated in its editorial, "Mr. Lincoln . . . has slowly and steadily risen in the respect, confidence, and admiration of the people."[10]

The *Washington Daily Morning Chronicle*'s lead story for the morning of March 4 spoke of vindication. "The reinauguration suggests the proud reflection that every prediction as to himself, made by the friends of the Union at the beginning of his Administration, has been confirmed." This second inauguration, so some of his supporters argued, ought to be a time for Lincoln to crow a bit. The *Daily Morning Chronicle* agreed. "We shall not be surprised if the President does not, in the words he will utter this morning, point to the pledges he gave us in his inaugural of 1861, and claim that he has not departed from them in a single substantial instance."[11] This kind of prose invited the president to speak a strong word about both his own personal success and the impending victory of union forces.

On Friday morning, March 3, visitors crowded the streets of the capital in spite of the inclement weather. The locals knew that spring arrives cautiously in Washington. In early March, the spring rains gently turn the grass from winter brown to green. Chestnuts and elms, planted at the turn of the century, were not quite in bloom. Cherry blossoms would not be known in the capital until early in the next century.

Nothing could hide the disorder and dirt that were everywhere. The national capital, scarcely six decades old, remained an almost-city. Charles Dickens, on his first visit to the United States, in 1842, had called the American capital "the City of Magnificent Intentions." He described Washington satirically as "spacious avenues, that begin in nothing, and lead nowhere; streets, mile-long, that only want houses, roads, and inhabitants; public buildings that need but a public to be complete."[12]

When Lincoln had come to Washington as a congressman from Illinois in December 1847, the city had barely thirty-five thousand residents. The 1860 census counted 61,400 inhabitants. Twelve cities ranked ahead of the capital in population. Most would add that these cities also surpassed the capital in civility and culture.

One visitor from Philadelphia was irked. "If you want to be disgusted with the place chosen for the Capital of your country, visit it in the spring time, near the close of four days' rain, when the frost is beginning to come out of the ground. Whatever other objects of interest may attract your notice, the muddy streets and pavements will scarcely escape you."[13]

The leading objects of interest in the capital were the Capitol building with its new iron dome, the Executive Mansion, the Library of Congress, the Post-Office, the Patent Office, and the Treasury. European visitors dismissed the White House as an ordinary country house. A great problem with the White House was its location near the Potomac Flats. This dismal body of water was held responsible for the outbreaks of malaria that occurred in summer and autumn. The Smithsonian Institution stood alone as a museum. A tour of all the important buildings in Washington could be done in an afternoon.

An alternative tour of Washington could *not* be completed in an afternoon. New residents were learning to use the low, pallid hospitals, teeming with wounded soldiers, as landmarks. Washington, which had been transformed into an armed camp in the early days of the war, had now become a gigantic hospital. White buildings and tents dotted the city. Many hospitals were new structures, like the Stanton Hospital at New Jersey Avenue and I Street. Others, such as the Douglass Hospital, had taken over former private mansions on Minnesota Row. Many of the forty or so hospitals were makeshift single-story wooden sheds. All were crowded. Often hundreds, sometimes thousands of wounded soldiers lay in adjoining beds.

The staggering number of wounded and dying could not be confined to what looked like hospitals. The sick and wounded could be found in hotels, warehouses, schools, and lodges of fraternal orders. Georgetown College was turned into a hospital. Many private homes took in the wounded.

Churches vied with each other as makeshift hospitals. Carpenters overlaid the pews with scantling, long thin pieces of wood. Floors were then set in place over the pews. Beneath this temporary flooring were stored the pulpit, hymnbooks, pew cushions, and other permanent furniture of the church. On Independence Day, 1862, some church bells could not be rung because the wounded lay beneath the bells.

Even conventional government buildings were conscripted to help house the wounded. The Patent Office held injured Union soldiers. Anyone who wanted to visit the Smithsonian could not miss the huge Armory Square Hospital nearby, which was in fact a series of parallel sheds. Even the Capitol building was transformed into a hospital, two thousand cots placed in corridors and even in the Rotunda.

———

On Friday, March 3, as the evening wore on, a dense fog descended over the capital, yet even the dismal weather could not dampen the spirits of the visitors. Many had traveled great distances to come to the inaugural events. That so many came from so far is captured in the press reports' continual use of the word "strangers" to describe the audience gathering for the inauguration ceremonies. Some strangers were allowed to spend the night in the halls of the Capitol in order to find protection from the rain.[14]

Among the evening arrivals were three fire companies from Philadelphia. Nearly three hundred men, dressed smartly in black fire hats, coats, and pants, and red shirts caught everyone's eyes. The capital became musical with military bands and serenaders. High in the fog, the lights of the now completed Capitol building created the effect of a halo over the festivities.

As for the government, there was no time yet for celebration. Lincoln met with his cabinet until a late hour, working to finish business related to the last acts of the outgoing 38th Congress. The Senate had been meeting all day and continued its session into the evening. In the middle of their session, driving rain rattled the windows in the Capitol building. As tempers flared and energy sagged, this legislative all-nighter became a strange prelude to the inaugural ceremonies on the morrow.

————

March 4 dawned with incessant rain. A large number of visitors, in order to avoid the difficulty of getting lodgings, had decided not to come until the day of the inauguration. They were arriving aboard special trains the railroad companies had prepared to accommodate them.

The streets oozed with soft mud, described by locals as "black plaster." The Corps of Engineers surveyed the scene to determine the practicality of laying pontoons on Pennsylvania Avenue from the Capitol to the White House. They found the bottom too unstable to hold the anchors of the needed boats. The project was abandoned. During the early-morning hours, gale winds whipped through the city, uprooting trees.

The Senate and House worked on until seven o'clock in the morning. On one occasion a sudden burst of rain suggested "an explosion inside the building," causing many "to run towards the doors." The leaders of the House and Senate convinced the members to come back to their seats, assuring them that the noise "was only a storm."[15]

In the early morning, fog continued to hang over the city as the crowd began arriving at the east entrance of the Capitol. Carriages were in great demand. Premium prices were being offered for rides to the proceedings. Police estimates placed the crowd between thirty and forty thousand. The *Philadelphia Inquirer* reported that the arriving throng was present "in force sufficient to have struck terror into the heart of Lee's army (had the umbrellas been muskets)."[16]

Seldon Connor, a Union soldier from Michigan who had arrived in Washington only the day before, was overwhelmed by the size of the gathering. He wrote to his mother, "There was a crowd almost numberless."[17] Maggie Lindsley, twenty-four, had been a supporter of the Union cause in Nashville, a view not shared by most of her friends. Encountering the crowds heading for the inaugural, she wrote later that day in her diary, "We were on the edge of a great surging ocean of humanity."[18] As visitors and residents walked toward the Capitol, they encountered military patrols on horseback at every major intersection.

Some in the crowd remembered back to quite a different scene four years earlier. Trepidation and gloom had clouded March 4, 1861. Everything seemed in disarray. Sections of the new iron Capitol dome lay jumbled near the inauguration stand, waiting for fitting. Just two weeks before, as Lincoln traveled from Illinois to Washington, he had to be spirited through Baltimore in disguise to avoid abduction on his way to assume the presidency. This episode, of which Lincoln was not proud, humiliated his supporters. Cartoonists ridiculed him, adding to the venom that was already spewing out in some of the press reports on the president-elect.

At that first inauguration, Confederate sympathizers were still everywhere in the capital. General Winfield Scott had stationed sharpshooters on the roofs of buildings along Pennsylvania Avenue. Two batteries of artillery were posted near the Capitol. The Capitol building rose above the gathering crowd, but it was incomplete, the arm of a crane sticking out to one side.

——

On the Saturday of the Second Inaugural, the rain stopped at nine-thirty. By ten-thirty, the skies were clearing. But at ten-forty, torrential rains came again. Open windows, crammed with sightseers, had to be "slammed shut." Women tied their white handkerchiefs to their bonnets. Ten inches of mud covered the unpaved avenues, making the proverbial filthy streets of Washington worse than usual. Noah Brooks, correspondent for the *Sacramento Daily Union,* wrote, "Flocks of women streamed around the Capitol, in most wretched plight; crinoline was smashed, skirts bedaubed, and moiré antique, velvet, laces and such dry goods were streaked with mud from end to end."[19] What should have been a brightly dressed gathering appeared instead thoroughly bedraggled by the elements of mud and wind. But the women and the men didn't seem to care. The reporter for the *New York Herald* reported, "The crowd was good-natured." They were there to participate in these grand events.[20]

The ceremonial procedures would not differ substantially from Lincoln's first inauguration. Yet there were differences. Instead of the small clusters of soldiers present in 1861, large numbers of military could be observed throughout the city. In certain sections of the capital, multiplying numbers of Confederate deserters could be seen. Twelve hundred and thirty-nine disheartened Confederate soldiers had arrived in February. All the soldiers were marked by their wounds. Amputation had become the trademark of Civil War surgery. According to federal records, three out of four operations were amputations. Too often the surgery had to be repeated. Many visitors professed shock at the sight of so many young men with amputated legs or arms.

Black soldiers changed the composition of the army from

1861 to 1865. For the first two years of the war, the Union Army was all white. Lincoln had initiated the North's employment of African-American troops when he issued the Emancipation Proclamation on January 1, 1863. The use of black troops prompted protests both in the North and in the South, but 179,000 black soldiers and ten thousand sailors would serve in the Union forces before the end of the war. Black soldiers had now become a common sight in Washington.

The presence of so many blacks in the inaugural crowds particularly struck the correspondent for the *Times* of London. He estimated that "at least half the multitude were colored people. It was remarked by everybody, stranger as well as natives, that there never had been such crowds of negroes in the capital." Whereas many in the crowds, because of the mud, were dressed in "old clothes." African Americans, despite the dismal weather, were noticeable also because of their dress "in festive reds, blues, and yellows, and very gaudy colors."[21]

By midmorning, the inaugural parade was forming. The parade preceded the ceremonies in Lincoln's time. Grand Marshal Ward Lamon, an old friend from Illinois, went to the White House to escort the president to the Capitol. Lamon had arranged to have thirteen brightly clothed United States marshals and thirteen citizen marshals accompany Lincoln's carriage. Lamon did not know that Lincoln had driven off to the Capitol earlier in the morning to sign some bills, abandoning the usual protocol for an inauguration. As one observer noted, the parade was "the play of Hamlet with Hamlet left out."[22]

The parade began to move at 11 A.M. from the corner of Pennsylvania Avenue and Tenth. Crowds thronged both sides of Pennsylvania Avenue. At the front marched 119 metropolitan policemen. Union soldiers, many in shabby blue uniforms, followed. The three companies of volunteer firemen from Philadelphia were a hit with their smart uniforms.

Chicago firemen drew their engine while they marched, as did companies from other cities. Local pride soared when the Fire Department of the City of Washington followed with its horse-drawn steam engines.

Far down the parade line was something never before witnessed at a presidential inauguration. Four companies of black soldiers, members of the 45th Regiment United States Colored Troops, marched smartly. Immediately following was a lodge of African-American Odd Fellows. The crowd cheered.

Next in line came a series of floats, patriotic but a bit dowdy. First was the Temple of Liberty, a tent made out of muslin. The muslin was by now soggy. The original intention had been to surround the tent with young "maidens" from each state of the Union. The rain prompted the float's organizers to replace the young girls with boys. The boys entertained the crowd by singing patriotic songs such as "Rally Round the Flag" and "The Battle Cry of Freedom." The next float—drawn by four white horses, soon spattered with mud—presented by members of the Lincoln-Johnson Club of East Washington, bore a replica of the iron warship *Monitor.*

The crowd buzzed as the third float came into view. A Gordon press had been installed. Staff members of the *Daily Morning Chronicle* busily printed a four-page inaugural newspaper that contained a program for the day, copies of which were tossed to the spectators on both sides of the avenue.

The special marshals and the President's Union Light Guard escorted Mrs. Lincoln. The crowd cheered the presidential coach along the route from the White House to the Capitol, not knowing that the president was not present.

After a festive beginning, the parade suddenly came to a halt in a snarled confusion of horses, troops, and fire engines. Following twenty minutes without movement, an impatient Mary Lincoln bypassed the parade and proceeded by a back way to the Capitol. The parade finally resumed, now without either the president or the president's wife.

———

On this inauguration day, Lincoln would see what no president before him had seen, the new iron dome of the Capitol towering above the crowd. The old wooden dome, first seen by Congressman Abraham Lincoln on his arrival in Washington in 1847, had been hauled down. In 1855, Congress committed itself to build a new dome, its design based on European traditions stretching back to the sixteenth century. The decoration of the dome, however, reflected the technology and taste of mid-nineteenth-century America. The taste for luxury meant that an "opulent overlay of ornament" characterized the decoration. The use of cast iron allowed for confident and complicated designs and decorations.[23]

When hostilities had begun, many questioned whether the renovation should go forward. How could one justify the expenditure of money and material, to say nothing of manpower, now that a civil war was breaking out? The work on the Capitol extensions and the dome stopped on May 15, 1861. Hundreds of workers were dismissed. They returned to their homes or joined regiments that were forming. Thousands of troops were quartered in the Capitol. Bakeries began operating in the basement rooms of the Library of Congress.[24]

Lincoln insisted that the work on the dome proceed. Continuing the construction of the dome, the central architectural symbol in the center of the nation's capital, came to symbolize that the Union was continuing. For Lincoln, the completion of the Capitol represented his hope that one day all the states and their representatives would meet again to do the nation's business beneath its new dome. As if on Union time, the radiant new iron dome of the Capitol was being completed just as the war to save the Union entered its final phase.[25]

Atop the Capitol dome stood *Armed Liberty.* Thomas Crawford, an American sculptor working in Rome, was invited in 1855 to come up with ideas for a statue for the top of the dome. Crawford offered a design that he entitled "Freedom triumphant in War and Peace." In January 1856, two photographs of sketches by Crawford were forwarded to the secretary of war, the Cabinet officer in the Pierce administration with ultimate responsibility for restoring the Capitol.

The secretary of war was Jefferson Davis. He was pleased with Crawford's sketch, except for one important feature. A feminine figure wore a cap, the symbol of the liberty of a freed slave in ancient Greece. Davis objected to this symbol "as the badge of the freed slave." The future president of the Confederate States of America observed, "Though it should have another emblematic meaning today, a recurrence to that origin may give it in the future the same popular acceptance which it had in the past." He suggested a helmet.[26]

The casting of *Armed Liberty* was to be done by sculptor Clark Mills at his foundry near Washington. Mills had achieved prominence for his equestrian statue of Andrew Jackson, dedicated in 1853 in Lafayette Square, near the White House. For casting *Armed Liberty,* Mills used Lake Superior copper and tin as the basic materials. Small amounts of zinc were mixed in to produce a rich bronze-green tint.

On December 2, 1863, *Armed Liberty* was placed upon the dome of the Capitol. This symbolic moment was sealed by a thirty-five-gun salute from the Capitol, which was answered by salutes from the twelve forts that ringed the city. *Armed Liberty* held a sword in one hand, symbolizing power, and a wreath of flowers in the other hand, signifying glory. This statue, a symbol of freedom in the form of a freed slave, would look down upon Abraham Lincoln at his second inauguration.[27]

Posters, ribbons, ferrotypes, medals, and tokens prepared for the 1864 presidential campaign were visible everywhere. One poster from the election campaign surely summed up the fervent sentiments of many arriving for the day's events:

All Who Are Opposed To A
DISGRACEFUL ARMISTICE With Traitors.

Surely Lincoln would articulate these sentiments in his eagerly awaited address.

One medal was inscribed "A Foe to Traitors," while another read "No Compromise with Armed Rebels." An 1864 campaign ribbon captured the now clearly understood twin goals of the war: "Union and Liberty." Another medal was inscribed "Freedom to All Men / War for the Union." The theme of human rights was captured in tokens. One side read "Lincoln," and on the other side was inscribed "Proclaim Liberty Throughout the Land." Another read "Lincoln and Liberty" on one side and, on the other, "Freedom/Justice/Truth."[28]

The Committee on Arrangements was taking measures to move the inaugural ceremonies into the Senate chamber, in case the weather didn't improve. A decision to do so would be a great disappointment to the tens of thousands massing outside. At ten o'clock, the Senate galleries had opened and spectators rushed to secure seats. The press gallery of the Senate was crowded with reporters from across the nation. Undaunted by the mud on their grand skirts, women were settled above the assemblage in the ladies' gallery.

On the Senate floor, senators conversed with government officials and celebrity guests. Many eyes were riveted on the military heroes Admiral David G. Farragut and General Joseph Hooker. The diplomatic corps was resplendent in uniforms replete with gold lace and decorations. The air grew muggy. The ventilating system of the Capitol was insufficient to deal with the moisture and humidity. As more and more people crowded the Senate floor and galleries in their rain-soaked clothes, the temperature rose.

At eleven-forty-five, the official procession began to file into the chamber. The retiring vice-president, Hannibal Hamlin, and the vice-president-elect, Andrew Johnson, walked in together. The reporter for the *New York Herald* observed that Johnson, leaning on Hamlin's arm, was unsteady, but concluded that the reason was excitement. Lincoln was still signing bills in the president's room just off the Senate chamber.

At twelve o'clock, Hamlin began his farewell speech. Hamlin was born in Maine in 1809 (the same year as Lincoln). His place on the Republican ticket in 1860 balanced a former Whig from the West with a former Democrat from New England. Hamlin disliked both slavery and abolitionists. Complaining that the vice-presidency was a powerless job, and that he was not consulted by Lincoln, Hamlin had spent increasing time away from Washington. He even served garrison duty with the Maine Coast Guard for two months in 1864.

Secretary of State William Seward and members of the Cabinet interrupted Hamlin's short speech as they arrived to take their seats. Next came the chief justice, Salmon P. Chase, leading in eight black-gowned old men, who took their places before the presiding officer's desk. Senators asked the vice-president to ask the women in the galleries to stop their "disrespectful giggling and chatter," but the request had no effect. Hamlin resumed his speech, only to be interrupted yet again when Mary Lincoln took her seat in the diplomatic gallery. Guests continued to arrive as he concluded.[29]

———

Andrew Johnson was introduced and rose to give his inaugural speech. Lincoln had left the choice of a vice-president to the convention at Baltimore. Johnson, a war Democrat from Tennessee, had been chosen as Lincoln's running mate to symbolize the transformation of the Republican Party in 1864 into a National Union party. Lincoln had admired Johnson's courage in adhering to the Union after his state seceded. In the nineteenth century, the vice-president commanded less stature and visibility than today. Accession to the presidency did not enter into Johnson's nomination, although two presidents, William Henry Harrison and Zachary Taylor, had died in office.

Lincoln arrived and took his seat in the Senate chamber just as Johnson began to speak. No one in the Senate chamber or gallery was aware of how Johnson had spent the hour before his speech. He had not been well for several weeks, and the trip from Nashville to Washington had only made things worse. The morning of the inauguration, he went to the vice-president's office in the Capitol to await the official ceremony. Feeling unwell, he asked for some whisky. He filled his glass and drank it straight. On the way to the Senate chamber he had another. And then a third.[30]

At the new vice-president's first utterance, it became obvious to all that Andy Johnson was drunk. The traditional brief inaugural speech of the vice-president became a rambling affair. Trumpeting that he had risen to this high office from the masses, he instructed all present that they owed their positions to the people. He did not even address the Cabinet members by their titles.

The assembled dignitaries and guests were shocked. The Republicans began to hang their heads. Attorney General James Speed whispered to Secretary of the Navy Gideon

Welles, "The man is certainly deranged." He then sat with his eyes closed. Welles in turn whispered to Stanton, "Johnson is either drunk or crazy."[31] The *New York Herald* later reported that Johnson delivered "a speech remarkable for its incoherence which brought a blush to the cheek of every senator and official of the government."[32] Johnson, scheduled to speak for seven minutes, spoke for seventeen. Finally, Hamlin pulled at Johnson's coat tail and the tribulation ended.

But not quite. After Johnson took the oath of office, he put his hand on the Bible and said in a blaring voice, "I kiss this Book in the face of my nation of the United States." He followed his words with a drunken kiss. Lincoln bent over to Senator John B. Henderson of Missouri, a marshall for the inauguration, and whispered, "Do not let Johnson speak outside."[33]

———

At eleven-forty the rain had suddenly ceased, and arrangements were completed to hold the ceremonies outside. A new procession of dignitaries was formed. President Lincoln was escorted through a corridor to the temporary wood platform that extended from the east front of the Capitol.

Clouds flounced across the sky, turning and twisting in the wind. Rifts in the clouds revealed an azure sky. Noah Brooks, who was Lincoln's friend as well as correspondent for the *Sacramento Daily Union,* described the immense crowd as a "sea of heads. As far as the eye could see, the throng looked like waves breaking at its outer edges."[34]

Soldiers were dispersed throughout the crowd. Some had come in uniform from the camps. Many more came from the hospitals in the Washington area. Lincoln was always the soldiers' president. He liked to mingle with enlisted men. He visited wounded soldiers in the hospitals. The military personnel had returned a 75 percent vote for him in his re-election the previous November. Now thousands of them were present to witness the inauguration of their president.

Noted Washington camera artist Alexander Gardner was poised to record the event for posterity. The Second Inaugural Address would be the only occasion on which Lincoln was photographed delivering a speech. Gardner's photographs, subject to the limitations of a craft and technology still in its young adulthood, were either limited by movements during the slow exposure or were simply out of focus. The photograph is so unfocused that Lincoln's face cannot be seen clearly.

In front of the president, in the crowd, Lincoln recognized Frederick Douglass, the articulate African-American abolitionist leader, reformer, and newspaper editor. Lincoln's First Inaugural Address had dismayed Douglass. He had found Lincoln's words much too conciliatory toward the South. Douglass visited Lincoln in the White House in 1863 and again in 1864 to speak with the president about a variety of issues concerning African Americans. Douglass's attitudes about the president during the Civil War had whipsawed back and forth from disgust to respect, and from despair to hope. Today, Douglass had come to hear what Lincoln would say now that the end of the war was in view.[35]

Up behind the right buttress stood the actor John Wilkes Booth. Lincoln had seen Booth perform at Ford's Theatre the previous November. Booth, twenty-six years old, had been an actor since he was seventeen. Seething with hatred, Booth had been working on a plan to abduct Lincoln and take him to Richmond. Now that the South's military fortunes had taken a turn for the worse, Booth resolved that stronger measures were needed. He was in touch with the Southern Secret Service as he sought an opportunity to do something "heroic" for the South. He came to hear the Second Inaugural for his own dark motives. He must have wanted to know, what would this false president say?

———

When Lincoln was introduced, the crowd exploded in expectation. Brooks reported, "A roar of applause shook the air, and again, and again repeated."[36] The military band played "Hail to the Chief," helping to build the enthusiasm of the gathering. The applause and cheers rolled toward those in the farthest reaches of the crowd. Finally, George T. Browne, sergeant-at-arms of the Senate, arose and bowed with black hat in hand, a signal for the crowd to become still.

Abraham Lincoln rose from his chair. He stepped from underneath the shelter of the Capitol building and out past the magnificent Corinthian columns. At fifty-six, he looked older than his years.

The president advanced to a white iron table made by Major Benjamin Brown French. Lincoln had appointed French commissioner of public buildings in 1861. In December 1864, French climbed onto the dome of the Capitol. Finding a single baluster left of the balustrade that surrounded the top of the inner dome, he decided to use it as the standard for a small table. French gathered up other pieces left over from construction and had the pieces brought to his home, where he fashioned "a very handsome and very solid table." He placed the table in his bay window to be admired by visitors. He planned to put the table in the garden in the summer.

On March 4, the French table was the single piece of furniture at the Second Inaugural. We do not know how it got there. It well may be that French, who was critical of many in Washington but was always admiring of Lincoln, offered it or simply placed it there himself. The small iron table symbolized for French the reuniting of the fragments of the Union.[37] On the table was a lone tumbler of water.

As Lincoln rose, he put on and adjusted his steel-rimmed eyeglasses. He held in his left hand his Second Inaugural Address, printed in two columns. The handwritten draft of the address had been set in type. The galley proof was clipped and pasted in an order to indicate pauses for emphasis and breathing.

Precisely as Lincoln began to speak, the sun broke through the clouds. Many persons, at the time and for years after, commented on this celestial phenomenon. Michael Shiner, an African-American mechanic in the naval shipyard in Washington, recorded his awe in his diary entry for March 4. "As soon as Mr. Lincoln came out the wind ceased blowing and the rain ceased raining and the Sun came out and it became clear as it could be and calm." Shiner continued, "A star made its appearance . . . over the Capitol and it shined just as bright as it could be." Brooks reported the same phenomenon. "Just at that moment the sun, which had been obscured all day, burst forth in its unclouded meridian splendor, and flooded the spectacle with glory and with light."[38]

Lincoln prepared to speak.

2

"At this second appearing . . ."

At this second appearing, to take the oath of the presidential office, there is less occasion for an extended address than there was at the first. Then a statement, somewhat in detail, of a course to be pursued, seemed fitting and proper. Now, at the expiration of four years, during which public declarations have been constantly called forth on every point and phase of the great contest which still absorbs the attention, and engrosses the enerergies [sic] of the nation, little that is new could be presented. The progress of our arms, upon which all else chiefly depends, is as well known to the public as to myself; and it is, I trust, reasonably satisfactory and encouraging to all. With high hope for the future, no prediction in regard to it is ventured.

Lincoln's opening words, *"At this second appearing,"* are not a throwaway line. Lincoln almost did not appear.

For much of Lincoln's first term, political pundits had predicted that he would be another of the one-term presidents that had become customary in the middle years of the nineteenth century. In the days before March 4, 1865, in a federal government that was only seventy-six years old, American as well as foreign newspapers much commented that this would be the first time in thirty-two years that a president would be inaugurated for a second term.[1]

The Republican Party had been cobbled together in 1854 from Whig, Free Soil, Democratic, and other parties and interests. Lincoln, who had served only a single term in the House of Representatives in the late 1840s, had first attracted national attention in 1858 as a result of his performance in his debates with Senator Stephen Douglas in Illinois.

Lincoln trailed William Seward 173½ to 102, with Salmon Chase third, on the first ballot for presidential candidate at the 1860 Republican convention. Seward, a senator and former governor from New York, and Chase, the governor of Ohio, were both better-known politicians. Lincoln was chosen as the Republican Party's presidential candidate on the third ballot. Critics were quick to point out that the nominating convention was held at Chicago, in Lincoln's home state of Illinois. (On the eve of his second inauguration, the *New York Herald* reminded its readers that Lincoln was elected "as a one-term compromise" by "cliques" within his party.[2]) Ever after, politicians gossiped that the relatively unknown Lincoln was put forward as an available compromise candidate in 1860.

In the midst of the elation of Lincoln's second inauguration, many could remember back a scant seven months to a quite different mood. In the summer of 1864, many of Lincoln's supporters were resigned to his having only one term. A mood of desolation pervaded the White House. Lincoln appeared weary, his lanky frame visibly sagging under the burdens of the presidency. Just a year after the decisive summer victories of '63 at Gettysburg and Vicksburg, the summer of 1864 witnessed campaigns that brought disappointment, even despair, throughout the North. In early May 1864, Grant began the year's Eastern campaign by confidently leading nearly a hundred thousand men against Lee's sixty-five thousand soldiers in the Battle of the Wilderness. In the fighting that lay ahead, at Spotsylvania and at Cold Harbor, Virginia, Grant would suffer almost sixty thousand casualties—nearly the equal of the troops Lee put in the field. By the end of seven weeks of battles and skirmishes, the Northern public began to ask if victory was worth the swelling cost in human lives.

As casualties escalated in the North, the cumulative effect of more than three years of war began taking its effect on the president, politicians, and the populace. Lincoln barely slept during the first week of the Battle of the Wilderness. Sherman was marching toward Atlanta, but the city still remained in rebel control. There were long silences when no one was quite sure of the progress of Sherman's campaign. Although Grant stood before Richmond, the reputation of Lee and his troops was still respected, if not feared. All the while, the casualties were mounting. By the early summer, casualty counts of two thousand a day were slackening the will to fight on.

With no major victories for more than a year now, weariness seemed to be winning out. Some Democrats began to press for a negotiated settlement to end the carnage. Even as the North was getting used to finding new generals to lead the war effort, some Republicans began to suggest it was time to find a new candidate for the presidential election coming in November 1864.

Lincoln was receiving pessimistic reports from his advisers about his prospects for re-election. Henry J. Raymond, founder of the *New York Times* and chairman of the Republican National Committee, convened the committee at the Astor House in New York on August 22. Raymond, a moderate Republican, had always been emphatic that the moral issue of slavery should be subordinated to the practical questions of political power. He admired Lincoln but had not been enthusiastic about the Emancipation Proclamation.

In early August 1864, after canvassing the situation with members representing all the states, he sat down to write the president. Raymond told Lincoln that even if an election were "to be held now in Illinois we should be beaten." Simon

Cameron, a key Pennsylvania leader and Lincoln's former secretary of war, reported, "Pennsylvania is against us." Raymond in turn declared that New York "would go 50,000 against us tomorrow."[3]

Why this dismal turn of events? Raymond, a friend and supporter of the president, wrote frankly about what he believed to be the problem: "the want of military successes, and the impression in some minds, the fear and suspicion in others, that we are not to have peace *in any event* under this Administration until Slavery is abandoned." Lincoln, for so long accused by abolitionists and radicals within his own party of going too slowly on slavery, was being indicted for holding his ground on the moral imperative of first restraining but now removing slavery. In sum, Raymond told Lincoln, "the tide is setting strongly against us."[4]

Lincoln became resigned in early August 1864 to not being re-elected. On August 23, 1864, six days before the Democratic convention would select his opponent, he wrote a private memorandum expressing his feelings. "This morning, as for some days past, it seems exceedingly probable that this administration will not be re-elected. Then it will be my duty to so cooperate with the President-elect as to save the Union between the election and the inauguration; as he will have secured his election on such ground that he cannot possibly save it afterwards."[5]

Lincoln brought his private memorandum to the Cabinet meeting that afternoon. He presented it to his colleagues, folded so that none of the text was visible, and asked each of them to sign the back of the document.

This mood of pessimism changed dramatically when news reached the North that Atlanta was evacuated on September 1 and that Sherman had led his troops into the city on September 2. A revival of Unionist fervor began to sweep through the North. Lincoln's spirits were buoyed. The change in the fortunes of battle helped Lincoln win the election against his Democratic opponent, General George McClellan, an overwhelming victory in electoral votes, 221 to 21 for McClellan. Lincoln received 2,203,831 votes to McClellan's 1,797,019 votes. He would approach his second inauguration vindicated personally, and expecting victory in the field.

———

Lincoln began his address in a subdued tone. In the highly charged atmosphere of wartime Washington, with soldiers everywhere, it is as if he wanted to lower anticipations. In the first, third, and fifth sentences of this first paragraph, Lincoln lowered them with the key words *"less . . . little . . . no."*

He started more like an observer than the main actor. The language of the first paragraph is impersonal. Yes, he used the pronouns *"I"* and *"myself,"* but the ethos of the paragraph was unemotional. Lincoln directed the focus of his remarks away from himself by speaking in a passive voice. Avoiding the active voice set up a paradigm that Lincoln followed throughout the address. After this first paragraph, he would use no more personal pronouns.

Lincoln dispensed one by one with the usual contents of such an address. In the first sentence he said that this was not the occasion for *"an extended address."* In the second sentence he reiterated why a detailed *"statement"* was proper four years before, but not today. In the third sentence he reminded the audience that on many other occasions they had heard *"public declarations"* on *"every point and phase"* of the war, implying that he would not make such a declaration on this occasion. The audience surely would have relished hearing the commander-in-chief give a report on *"the progress of our arms,"* but he would not do that.

After Lincoln told the audience everything the speech would not be, he concluded the first paragraph by announcing he was offering *"no prediction"* about the end of the war. The problem, as Lincoln realized, was that predictions had been made all too often in the first years of the war. Predictions led to false optimism that had again and again led to disappointments.

There seems to be nothing in Lincoln's beginning paragraph that would arouse the passions of the audience. The opening, unlike either the First Inaugural or the Gettysburg Address, contains no creative stylistic flourishes. When we first hear or read the beginning words of Lincoln's Second Inaugural, they may even come upon us as awkward, if not ungraceful.

In these initial words Lincoln did not seem to build bridges to the aspirations of his Union audience. The audience was surely waiting to hear the re-elected president give voice to their feelings of victory, with the end of the war in sight. His supporters hoped he would speak of the personal vindication of being re-elected. Lincoln's beginning seems, at first glance, to undercut the grand opportunity of a second inaugural address. After thirty-two years during which no president had been elected for a second term, Lincoln could only muster: *"At this second appearing."*

———

The text of the Second Inaugural consists of 703 words. Lincoln arranged his words in twenty-five sentences in four paragraphs. Five hundred and five words in the address are of one syllable.

Lincoln's pattern was to read his addresses slowly. He usually spoke barely more than one hundred words per minute. At this rate, even incorporating applause, it probably took him only six or seven minutes to deliver the Second Inaugural Address.

We have the record of but a single voice reporting on the

composition of the text. Francis B. Carpenter, an artist who spent six months in residence at the White House, related a conversation with Lincoln on the previous Sunday evening, February 26. Carpenter was sitting in Lincoln's office in the Executive Mansion with two men from New York and Ohio who had arrived for an appointment with the president. He reported that the president came in by a side passage, only recently constructed, "holding in his hand a roll of manuscripts." Upon encountering Carpenter, the president exclaimed, "Lots of wisdom in that document, I suspect. It is what will be called my second inaugural, containing about six hundred words. I will put it in my drawer until I want it."[6] Then, seating himself by the fire, Lincoln spoke of the old days in Illinois.

The fact that Lincoln put the Second Inaugural in his drawer six days in advance of its delivery matches what we know about his writing. Lincoln took great pains in preparing his most important public addresses. Before his House Divided Speech (1858) and Cooper Union Address (1860), all his speeches were extemporaneous, sometimes aided by notes. As president, despite his reputation as an effective stump speaker, Lincoln did not trust himself in spontaneous situations where he was suddenly called upon to speak. More and more he declined these invitations. When he knew he was to present an important speech, he toiled far ahead.

In the Executive Mansion, Lincoln usually wrote his speeches first with pencil on stiff sheets of white pasteboard or boxboard. Noah Brooks tells of observing Lincoln writing in his armchair, his favorite position, with his legs crossed. He laid the sheets, which were five to six inches wide, on his knee. He crossed out words and edited until the text was ready to copy as the final version of the speech to be delivered.[7]

Although comfortable in a solitary approach to writing, Lincoln was not above seeking the opinions and editing of others. In preparing the First Inaugural, he received the help of a number of colleagues, especially Secretary of State–Elect William Seward.

We do not know about any editors in the construction of the Second Inaugural. Given Lincoln's own estimate that the length of the address was six hundred words as of February 26, it may be that he continued to revise and add. We have no record of his continuing efforts.

The Second Inaugural Address was handwritten in two columns on what was called foolscap, a form of paper approximately thirteen and a half by seventeen inches in size. The handwritten text reveals that Lincoln made only three corrections to the original text (see appendix I). The draft of the address was then set in type, the galley proof clipped and pasted on white boards.

The word "text" comes from the Greek root *teks,* which means "to weave." "Text" suggests "textile," or a fabric woven with many strands. Behind the printed text is an intricate weaving of meaning. Even when we refer to Lincoln's pruning down his earlier, more bombastic speech to the plainer style of Gettysburg or the Second Inaugural, "plain" is not meant to connote simple. Lincoln was chided early on in his presidency as a "Simple Susan," suggesting that his plain talk and one-syllable words had little meaning. Yes, the text of the Second Inaugural is in mostly one-syllable words, but the brilliance of Lincoln's words is in the weaving.[8]

Lincoln wrote primarily to be heard. He crafted his speeches as much for the ear as for the eye. Of course he expected his fellow citizens would read the address, often weeks or even months later, but this did not take away from his desire to craft a speech to be heard.

Before turning to an interpretation and analysis of the text, take the six to seven minutes required to read the address. Even better, speak it aloud, slowly, as Lincoln surely had done. Hear the way this weaving of meaning sounds to the ear.

————

As the audience was listening to the beginning paragraph, Lincoln saw his speech whole. In this first paragraph he was putting into place a pattern of organization for the full speech. He established an alignment divided into past, present, and future time. These three time tenses would become one of the organizing structures of the whole speech.

Lincoln's major addresses, including the House Divided Speech, the Cooper Union Address, and the Gettysburg Address, all possess what rhetorician Michael Leff calls "temporal markers."[9] This same design is present in the Second Inaugural. Lincoln's use of time directs the rhetorical movement of each of these speeches.

One of the problems in analyzing any of these speeches has been the tendency to focus upon only one unit or passage, to the neglect of the artistic whole. This tendency has only increased as television coverage has focused on only one passage or even only one sentence. The House Divided Speech in 1858 actually invoked the ire of many Republicans, who believed Lincoln was predicting a civil war. Lincoln was upset that they had not read the whole speech. The remembrance of the Second Inaugural has tended to emphasize two sections. The quotation used most frequently is the opening words of the last paragraph: *"with malice toward none; with charity for all."* Since the 1960s, the civil-rights struggle has focused more attention on the issue of slavery. Thus, in recent years, the forceful sentence from the third paragraph that begins, *"If we shall suppose that American Slavery is one of those offences,"* has been emphasized.

The problem with an analysis that focuses on one or two passages in a speech is that the framework of the whole is ignored. Most often the last paragraph of the Second Inaugural is quoted without reference to the whole, or the first and second paragraphs are ignored. We need to understand Lincoln's strategy for the complete speech.

———

We may ask, what were the expectations of second inaugural addresses? Granting the distinctiveness of March 4, 1865, how do Lincoln's words compare with the beginning paragraphs of other second inaugurals?

George Washington, in 1793, delivered the shortest second inaugural, 135 words. Washington did not deliver a speech. He simply acknowledged his re-election.

Thomas Jefferson, in 1805, began his Second Inaugural Address in an upbeat manner: "It is my duty to express the deep sense I entertain of this new proof of confidence from my fellow-citizens at large, and the zeal with which it inspires me to conduct."[10] Jefferson struck a note of confidence, surely a motif that Lincoln could lift up at the beginning of his Second Inaugural.

James Madison, in 1813, sounded two notes that would become commonplace in most succeeding second inaugural addresses: the confidence of the electorate in the re-elected president, and the importance of the times in which the president serves. Madison thanked the people for the "evidence that my faithful endeavors to discharge my arduous duties have been favorably estimated," and pointed to "the momentous period at which the trust has been renewed."[11]

James Monroe, in 1821, glowed with self-assurance as he began his Second Inaugural Address. "I shall not attempt to describe the grateful emotions which the new and very distinguished proof of the confidence of my fellow-citizens evinced in my re-election to this high trust, has excited in my bosom."[12] The irony of Monroe's gratitude is that he won re-election in a period when there was only one party in American politics. In this "Era of Good Feelings," the vote in the electoral college was 231 for Monroe, 1 vote for John Quincy Adams, and 3 who did not vote.

The closest historical comparison for the audience would be the last president before Lincoln to be re-elected. Andrew Jackson used the first paragraph of his Second Inaugural to thank the American people "for their approbation of my public conduct through a period which has not been without its difficulties." He went on to add, "I am at a loss for terms adequate to the expression of my gratitude."[13] Obviously, Jackson's literary humility can just as easily be seen as a way of magnifying himself and his own accomplishments.

Franklin D. Roosevelt is judged by many to be the greatest president to follow Lincoln. Roosevelt's presidency became known first for doing battle with the greatest economic depression in the nation's history. He began his Second Inaugural in 1937 by offering a recapitulation of the problem and a progress report on the pathway to victory.

> When four years ago we met to inaugurate a President, the Republic, single-minded in anxiety, stood in spirit here. We dedicated ourselves to the fulfillment of a vision—to speed the time when there would be for all the people that security and peace essential to the pursuit of happiness. We of the Republic pledged ourselves to drive from the temple of our ancient faith those who had profaned it; to end by action, tireless and unafraid, the stagnation and despair of that day. We did those things first.[14]

Although the language is an inclusive "we," Roosevelt steeps his words in a strong sense of personal triumph.

Jefferson, Madison, Monroe, Jackson, and Roosevelt insert themselves immediately into the structure of their second inaugural addresses. There is a marked contrast between the use of the personal pronoun by these five presidents and Lincoln. Jefferson works with the motif of the confidence of the people, but he is plainly saying that his leadership has justified their confidence. In the second sentence of their second inaugurals, Madison and Jackson emphasized that the electorate had lauded their efforts. Roosevelt, the commander-in-chief in a great domestic battle, assumed to himself a spirit of victory and vindication.

Jefferson, Madison, Jackson, and Roosevelt began their second inaugurals in personal and forceful prose that was clearly intended to raise expectations. Lincoln chose to be silent about thanking the voters for returning him to office. The "difficulties" that Jackson had been called upon to face seem pallid compared to Lincoln's four years of travail.

———

"At this second appearing," we pause to ask, how did Lincoln actually appear?

Recent debates over how to portray Franklin Delano Roosevelt in the monument to him in Washington, D.C., reveal how his paralysis was shielded from public view for the more than twelve years of his presidency. Many Americans did not know that the man who exuded such strength and energy struggled every day of his presidency merely to stand up.[15]

Lincoln was impossible to shield. Six feet four inches tall, he stood out above any crowd. From the beginning of his political career, Lincoln's appearance was a topic of conversation among both friends and enemies. His political handlers sought to make much of his appearance in his run for the presidency. His opponents used his appearance to deride him. George B. McClellan, Union general and Lincoln's opponent in the 1864 presidential election, called Lincoln "the Gorilla." Lincoln had been called worse.[16]

Ken Burns's 1990 documentary on the Civil War helped reintroduce Lincoln to more than twenty million television viewers. In the first war to be photographed, the photographs and images of Lincoln, although often in the background, were nonetheless pivotal among the countless images of soldiers and death.

Throughout Lincoln's life, one reason for the public's initial low expectations of him was its first glance at his form and features. More than a century later, when our image of Lincoln is through photographers who formalized him, we don't forget the remarkable appearance of the sixteenth president of the United States. Hailed after his death as the American everyman, he was the object of frequent ridicule during his political life.

Lincoln's public persona elicited comment even across the Atlantic. An English magazine reported in 1862: "To say he is ugly is nothing; to add that his figure is grotesque is to convey no adequate impression. Fancy a man almost six feet high, and thin in proportion, with long bony arms and legs which somehow always seem to be in the way." The writer then zeroes in on Lincoln's head and face. "Add to this figure a head, cocanut [sic] shaped, and somewhat too small for such a stature, covered with rough, uncombed hair, that stands out in every direction at once; a face, furrowed, wrinkled, and indented as though it had been scarred by vitriol."[17]

———

Lincoln's law partner, Billy Herndon, made it his mission in life to tell the story of the real Lincoln. Herndon, aghast at biographers who painted an idealized portrait of a Lincoln he never knew, wanted to set the record straight. Part of the real Lincoln for Herndon was his physical appearance. Herndon went into grand detail in describing him. "He was thin, wiry, sinewy, raw-boned; standing, he leaned forward—was what may be called stoop-shouldered, inclining to the consumptive by build." Herndon described Lincoln's face from the long association of viewing his associate in their law offices in Springfield. "His head ran backwards, his forehead rising as it ran back at a low angle. His hair was dark, almost black, and lay floating where his fingers or the winds left it, piled up and random." And again, "His ears were large, and ran out almost at right angles from his head, caused partly by heavy hats and partly by nature."

Herndon's earthy language went beyond physical description. "His structure was loose and leathery; his body was shrunk and shriveled; he had dark skin, dark hair, and looked woe-struck." For Herndon the physical was linked to the mental. What better way to grasp Lincoln's deliberate nature than to hear Herndon say: "The whole man, body and mind, worked slowly, as if it needed oiling"? What did all of this add up to for Herndon? "He was not a pretty man by any means, nor was he an ugly one; he was a homely man, careless of his looks, plain-looking and plain-acting."[18] Herndon's Lincoln was a rough-hewn product of the Western frontier.

———

Walt Whitman approached Lincoln from a different angle of vision. Whitman, who was just becoming known in the 1850s for the first editions of *Leaves of Grass,* branded the three presidents before Lincoln—Fillmore, Pierce, and Buchanan—"our topmost warning and shame." In 1856, Whitman wrote a tract entitled "The Eighteenth Presidency" that railed against the powers in political office. Read today, the language appears emotional and violent. Early on, Whitman asks where these politicians come from. He answers in epithets. "From the President's house, the jail, the venereal hospital . . . from the tumors and abscesses of the land; from the skeletons and skulls in the vaults of federal almshouses, from the running sores of the great cities." Whitman completed the pamphlet, set it in type, and offered proof sheets to editors and "rich persons" for publication. He had no takers. For more than seventy years, the yellowing proof sheets remained unpublished and forgotten.[19]

In his tract, Whitman saw in the distance rays of hope residing in the people. The eighteenth president would be a man of the people. He would right the moral and political wrongs of the nation. Whitman dared to hope for some "healthy-bodied, middle-aged, beard-faced American blacksmith or boatman" who would "come down from the West across the Alleghenies, and walk into the Presidency."[20]

Whitman experienced an epiphany on first seeing Lincoln in February 1861. The president-elect was on a circuitous twelve-day itinerary to Washington, D.C., for his inauguration. Threats were present everywhere along the route. He arrived on February 18 in New York City, a city where less than 35 percent had voted for him. Whitman was certain that, in the crowd of thirty thousand, "many an assassin's knife and pistol lurk'd in hip or breast-pocket there, ready, as soon as break and riot came." Lincoln arrived by hack at the Astor House Hotel. From the top of a stalled omnibus, Whitman marveled at the sight of this tall and ungraceful man in a black suit and a stovepipe hat. "I had, I say, a capital view of it all . . . his look and gait—his perfect composure and coolness—his unusual and uncouth height."[21]

After Whitman moved to Washington, D.C., in 1863, he observed Lincoln many times. He wrote in his notebook on August 12, 1863, "I see the President almost every day." Although Whitman never met Lincoln, "we have got so that we exchange bows, and very cordial ones." From these close encounters Whitman began to study Lincoln with great care and appreciation.

———

Photography and Lincoln were made for each other. The face of Lincoln, photographed by Mathew Brady and his pupil Alexander Gardner, brought the American public closer to their president than ever before. We know Washington and Jefferson only through stylized art based on European forms. The pre-presidential photography of Lincoln reveals the more homespun Western man whose clothes never quite seemed to fit.

Modern exhibits on Lincoln invariably display photographs that depict his unusual face and features. Especially poignant is the striking way Lincoln's face changes through the Civil War years. He came to describe himself as an old man by the time he left Springfield for Washington on the day before his fifty-second birthday. Photography allows us to see this remarkable aging process in Lincoln.

From Whitman's repeated sightings of Lincoln, he concluded that, in this new age of photography, "none of the artists or pictures has caught the deep though subtle and indirect expression of this man's face." Yes, Brady and Gardner were the best of their trade, but even their photographs of Lincoln did not fully capture the deep interior soul of his being. Whitman, after his initial enthusiasm with photography, quickly realized that this new visual art did not equal reality either. Whitman recognized that Lincoln, the Western man, was not like other politicians. Unfortunately, in the hands of photographers Brady and Gardner, Lincoln was dressed and posed like any other politician.

In a letter from Washington in 1863, Whitman attempted

to describe the citizen president. "I see very plainly ABRAHAM LINCOLN's dark brown face, with deep-cut lines, the eyes, always to me with a deep latent sadness in their expression."[22] On another occasion, after viewing Lincoln, Whitman wrote of Lincoln's face, "Of technical beauty it had nothing—but to the eye of a great artist it furnished a rare study, a feast, and fascination."

Whitman's eye was becoming more practiced as he worked as a nurse in the hospitals of Washington. He struggled to find a comparison to Lincoln's face. So filled with care and sorrow, Lincoln's face was a paradox. At last, Whitman wrote, "He has a face like a hoosier Michel Angelo, so awful ugly it becomes beautiful."[23]

———

In the first paragraph of his Second Inaugural Address, Lincoln mentioned everything he would *not* say. This approach must have been preparing us for something that was not yet obvious. Lincoln was opening the door to a very different kind of address from what was usual on such occasions.

Lincoln's apparently flat recital of chronology was actually preparing the ground for a profound conversation about historical causation. He had been carrying on this conversation in private musings, in interviews at the White House, and in letters, but never before in any extended way in a public address. Beginning with a recital of temporal signposts, as he had earlier at Cooper Union and at Gettysburg, Lincoln would ask his audience to think with him about the cause and meaning of the war.

3

"And the war came."

On the occasion corresponding to this four years ago, all thoughts were anxiously directed to an impending civil war. All dreaded it—all sought to avert it. While the inaugeral [sic] address was being delivered from this place, devoted altogether to saving the Union without war, insurgent agents were in the city seeking to destroy it without war—seeking to dissole [sic] the Union, and divide effects, by negotiation. Both parties deprecated war; but one of them would make war rather than let the nation survive; and the other would accept war rather than let it perish. And the war came.

As an undergraduate at UCLA, I was introduced to United States history in a course that used Vernon Louis Parrington's *Main Currents in American Thought* as the basic text. Parrington set himself the task of writing a history of the literary aspects of American politics. As a historian growing up in the Progressive Era, Parrington held strong opinions about heroes and villains who had advanced or retarded his progressive, secular vision.[1]

When Parrington came to Lincoln, he considered this man out of the West to be a splendid leader, but averred, "Few men who have risen to enduring eloquence have been so little indebted to rhetoric." He went on to describe Lincoln's speaking style: "His usual style was plain homespun, clear and convincing, but bare of imagery and lacking distinction of phrase."[2] For good or ill, Parrington's characterization of Lincoln as a public speaker did not make a lasting impression on this college sophomore.

The "plain homespun" depiction of Lincoln as speaker has had remarkable staying power. "Plain homespun" dogged Lincoln as he rose to be president, persisted in responses to Gettysburg and the Second Inaugural, and continued after his death. The characterization "plain homespun" was used both to praise and to castigate. Advocates used such imagery to champion Lincoln as the simple, sincere Western man. After Gettysburg, Lincoln was forever contrasted with Edward Everett and his high-toned oratory. Lincoln's detractors used the same imagery to demean the substance and depth of his rhetoric. Both miss the mark. Parrington's judgment, "lacking distinction of phrase," does not take the measure of Lincoln's artistry with words. An examination of his major speeches reveals Lincoln's masterful understanding and use of both imagery and distinctive phrase.

———

In the second paragraph, Lincoln began the shift in content and tone that would give this address its singular meaning. His artistry starts to be revealed. In a paragraph of five sentences, he employed several rhetorical strategies that work to guide and aid the listener.

First, Lincoln's central, overarching strategy was to emphasize common actions and emotions. In this paragraph he used *"all"* and *"both"* to be inclusive of North and South. Lincoln was here laying the groundwork for a theme that he would develop more dynamically in paragraphs three and four of his address.

Notice the subjects and adjectives in three of the five sentences in the second paragraph (emphasis is mine).

Sentence one: *"All thoughts were anxiously directed to an impending civil war."*

Sentence two: *"All dreaded it—all sought to avert it."*

Sentence four: *"Both parties deprecated war."*

Second, Lincoln balanced the use of these shared attitudes by acknowledging divisions. His rhetorical strategy here was the use of antithesis. In recalling events at the time of the First Inaugural Address, Lincoln employed two sets of antitheses:

Inaugural address . . .	*Insurgent agents . . .*
devoted altogether to <u>saving</u>	*seeking to <u>destroy</u> it*
the Union without war . . .	*without war . . .*
One of them would <u>make</u> war	*the other would <u>accept</u> war*
rather than let the nation survive.	*rather than let it perish.*

Contemporary correspondents reported that the audience applauded when Lincoln spoke of these divisions. He is at his most partisan in this early moment in the speech.

Some commentators have suggested that these antitheses diminish the theme of unity that Lincoln has just advanced and would later build upon. Yes and no. Yes, this was the most argumentative that Lincoln got in the Second Inaugural. He did frame his argument in terms of two parties. No, these antitheses are remarkably tame. Even the depiction of division, less pronounced than in the First Inaugural, is muted here. The strongest words he uses are *"insurgent agents."* Many in the crowd would have applauded more loudly if he had used words such as "Confederates," "rebels," or "traitors." The majority of the language is generic: *"all," "both," "parties," "one,"* and *"other."* Lincoln chose words that would not inflame his already anxious audience.

Third, Lincoln used the word *"war"* seven times. The image of *"war"* is actually present nine times in the ninety-nine words of the paragraph, for *"war"* is understood twice in the second sentence in two pronouns (emphasis is mine), *"All dreaded <u>it</u>—all sought to avoid <u>it.</u>"* I believe he repeated the image of *"war"* for both emphasis and movement.[3] The centrality of war is magnified, because the word is voiced in every sentence. The tension mounts throughout the paragraph, building to a crescendo in the three parts of the forceful third sentence:

> *(1) Both . . . deprecated war;*
> *(2) one . . . would <u>make</u> war;   (3) the other would <u>accept</u> war.*

In lifting up the word *"war,"* Lincoln was preparing his audience for more profound questions. Up until now, *"war"* was being described as the direct object, both grammatically and historically, of the principal actors. Now, recounting the complex motivations that led to war, Lincoln was beginning to suggest that neither side was fully in control. *"War"* was about to become the subject rather than the object.

Fourth, Lincoln used one of his favorite rhetorical devices: alliteration. He used "d" as the beginning letter in eight vital words:

> *directed*
> *dreaded*
> *delivered*
> *devoted*
> *destroy*
> *dissolve*
> *divide*
> *deprecated*

The use of alliteration, present in every sentence but the four-word last sentence, *"And the war came,"* promoted connection within the paragraph. Alliteration accented the rhythmic pacing of language. Finally, the repetition enhanced the cadence of Lincoln's words.

In this transitional paragraph, Lincoln started with history. Still speaking as if he were a chronicler, he took the assembled audience back to the thoughts and actions in the nation's capital four years before. In this reminder, Lincoln continued to direct attention away from himself. Instead of saying, "While I was delivering my inaugural address," he says in a passive mode, *"While the inaugural address was being delivered from this place."*

The deeper purpose of the paragraph is a discussion of the historical roots of the Civil War. In asking "who" started the war, Lincoln knew he was entering into territory fraught with problems. The way he asked and answered the question would signal the trajectory of his address.

Lincoln here followed his penchant for beginning speeches with historical perspective. I believe he did so for two reasons. First, he almost always sought to ground himself in history. In the speech that brought him local fame, the Address Before the Young Men's Lyceum of Springfield in 1838, Lincoln located the peculiar problems faced by his generation in a larger historical frame. "In the great journal of things happening under the sun, we, the American People, find our account running, under date of the nineteenth century of the Christian era."[4] The analogy of the account was a well-understood Christian image pointing toward stewardship. Here Lincoln pointed forward to the stewardship for the perpetuation of political institutions that would be the focus of the address.

In the speech that brought him national fame, the Address at Cooper Union in New York in February 1860, Lincoln's long introduction achieved its power from his meticulous grasp of historical data. Lincoln built his whole speech around a statement by Senator Stephen Douglas, "Our fathers, when they framed the Government under which we live, understood this question just as well, and even better, than we do now." The question under discussion was slavery. More precisely, "Does the proper division of local from federal authority, or anything in the Constitution, forbid our Federal Government to control as to slavery in our Federal Territories?" Republicans and Democrats divided over the answer to this question. Douglas answered in the affirmative, Lincoln in the negative.

The way Lincoln went about refuting Douglas and the Democrats held his audience spellbound. He began by identifying the thirty-nine "fathers" who voted for the Constitution at the Constitutional Convention in 1787. He then asked how these thirty-nine had expressed their understanding about the expansion of slavery into the territories in both previous and subsequent years. He enumerated the persons speaking and voting: four in 1784, two in 1787, seventeen in 1789, three in 1798, two in 1804, and two in 1819–20. Some persons voted more than once. In sum, he found twenty-three made choices regarding this question, with no evidence of the other sixteen's acting in any way. Twenty-one of the twenty-three acted consistently under the belief that the federal government did have the right to control slavery in the territories. In this remarkable *tour de force*, Lincoln used Douglas's words and his own historical detective work to argue from history for the present prohibition of the extension of slavery.

Lincoln was convinced that an excellent way to persuade people was to show them historical precedent. After 1854, Lincoln used Thomas Jefferson and the Declaration of Independence as the historical precedent upon which to ground his arguments for political equality for black Americans.

One can imagine the intense emotions at Gettysburg as people gathered for the dedication in November 1863. This was not a serene cemetery with rows of white crosses on manicured lawns. Gettysburg on that day was still an unfinished burial site. Barely a third of the bodies had been buried. Confederate skeletons lay unburied beneath stones and vegetation dying with the onset of winter.[5]

Lincoln placed this signal battle of the war in a larger historical context with an opening sentence that every schoolchild memorizes. "Fourscore and seven years ago our fathers brought forth on this continent a new nation conceived in liberty and dedicated to the proposition that all men are created equal."[6] In the intense present, Lincoln began in the past.

How did Lincoln develop such rhetorical creativity and skill? He never took time to explain his rhetorical theory or practice. I believe he did leave some rough drafts of a map, as it were, with some roads and junctions sketched in that we can attempt to follow.

In appreciating Lincoln's rhetorical genius, it would be easy to forget how much he changed and developed as a speaker. The fifty-six-year-old president who delivered his Second Inaugural Address in 1865 worked with a quite different rhetorical arsenal from that of the young man of twenty-eight who delivered the Young Men's Lyceum Address at Springfield in 1838. Into the 1850s, Lincoln used bombast, satire, and ridicule in speeches and debates. He could "take the hide off" his opponents in partisan speeches. When he came to Washington as president, even Lincoln's friends wondered if he would leave his barnyard similes back in Illinois.

His invective could be ham-fisted. In 1842, when Lincoln was thirty-three, in an anonymous letter to the local *Sangamo Journal,* he made fun of James A. Shields, the state auditor and a Democrat. Shields did not find it funny at all. He challenged Lincoln to a duel. Asked about the weapons that might be used in the confrontation, Lincoln was said to have suggested, "How about cow dung at five paces?" Preparations for the duel went forward, but wiser counsel prevailed. Lincoln looked back on this incident with embarrassment—at having allowed himself to be ruled by disorderly emotions instead of ordered reason.[7]

Lincoln worked hard to master a wide range of rhetorical abilities. One way to appreciate the changes in his more mature skills exhibited in the Second Inaugural will be to keep his earlier speeches within hearing distance.

———

We need to recall that Lincoln's formal schooling consisted of only two brief periods in an "A.B.C. school" in Kentucky. He looked back on his brief formal education and described it as "by littles." In 1858, Charles Lanman was preparing a *Dictionary of Congress*. He sent to all former members of Congress a request for information about their lives. Lincoln returned a forty-nine-word autobiography. When he came to the place on the questionnaire to list his education, perhaps he thought about his colleagues who were graduates of Harvard, Yale, and other colleges. He sent back to Lanman this description of his education: "defective."[8]

Lacking formal instruction, Lincoln worked all his life to become an educated person. He walked miles across the prairie as a youth to borrow a book to satisfy his love of learning. He taught himself Euclid's geometric principles while tramping around the Eighth Circuit as a lawyer because he wanted to discipline his mind. An earlier intention to lift up Lincoln as a man of the people unintentionally downgraded Lincoln as a thoughtful man of ideas. The recent emphasis on Lincoln as an astute politician should not be at the expense of de-emphasizing his philosophical or theological interests.

He wrote about his efforts to educate himself in an autobiographical sketch he prepared for John L. Scripps, who was writing a campaign biography in the summer of 1860. In his early twenties, Lincoln walked six miles to get a copy of Samuel Kirkham's *English Grammar*. He gained a thorough understanding of its contents, committing large parts to memory. Later, when John Calhoun, the newly appointed county surveyor, invited him to be his assistant, Lincoln studied Abel Flint's *System of Geometry and Trigonometry with a Treatise on Surveying.*[9]

When Lincoln arrived for his first term in the Illinois state legislature in 1834, he saw that many of the leading politicians were lawyers. He decided that he needed to study law. His friend and fellow legislator John Todd Stuart offered to help him and loaned him books. Although in later years a number of persons attempted to take credit for helping to educate him, Lincoln always liked to emphasize his self-education. He spoke of himself in the third person in this autobiography: "He studied with nobody."[10]

To be sure, Lincoln was good at using to his advantage self-deprecation regarding his education. He especially favored this tactic in his running interchanges with Douglas that would finally result in the debates of the summer of 1858. In one interchange, Lincoln said of himself, "I am not master of language; I have not a fine education; I am not capable of entering into a disquisition upon dialectics, as I believe you call it." Here Lincoln courted the sympathy of a Western crowd with self-disparaging language. The phrase about "dialectics" gave away another favorite Lincoln tactic. In this case he spoofed his "learned opponent."[11]

Moreover, Lincoln's speeches were Lincoln's speeches. He worked without speechwriters or ghostwriters. Often he worked without benefit of any advice or counsel from colleagues and friends. The First Inaugural is a notable exception. We have no evidence of any editorial counsel in the preparation of the Second Inaugural Address.

————

Lincoln grew to maturity in a culture that put a priority on the spoken word. He learned how to be heard in that culture. Whether he was addressing the Young Men's Lyceum of Springfield in 1838, or debating Stephen Douglas in 1858, both friend and foe came to respect his rhetorical skills. Whether speaking on behalf of himself or others, Lincoln learned early how to persuade an audience that would vote with their feet if they did not like the speaker's manner or content.

The young Illinois politician rose to popularity as a speaker. Even after he began to establish himself as a politician and lawyer, his abilities as a speaker set him apart from colleagues and rivals. A culture oriented around the spoken word rewarded those who learned its ways. Lincoln refined his oral skills not only at political rallies but also in numerous courthouses throughout Illinois. All interested in Lincoln are indebted to the Lincoln Legal Project, which has tracked down his legal briefs from around the state. Over five thousand legal documents have been published. We can understand more clearly how Lincoln's legal practice helped prepare him for politics and the presidency. These legal papers can also help us understand Lincoln's development as speaker and writer. The caution, however, is that no legal brief can capture the dynamism of Lincoln arguing in courts across Illinois.

Some might argue that the explosion of newspapers in pre–Civil War America militates against this contention of the priority of the spoken word. We need to remember, however, one of the functions of newspapers: they routinely printed the complete texts of political speeches. It should quickly be added that politicians did not hand complete manuscripts to the newspapers. Rather, the newspapers dispatched reporters who were adept at stenography. They wrote the speeches down in shorthand.

Up until the late 1850s, all of Lincoln's speeches were extemporaneous. He used notes but never a manuscript. The House Divided Speech in 1858 was the first time Lincoln used a manuscript. He would also use a manuscript at the Cooper Union Address, at Gettysburg, and in the two inaugural addresses.

Lincoln's practice regarding the printing of his speeches attests to the priority he gave to the spoken word. After he delivered his Cooper Institute Address in New York in February 1860, he went over to the *New York Herald* offices that evening to check the proofs of the reporter's version. Lincoln routinely checked on the transcripts of his speeches, though not to embellish them. His intent in checking a reporter's version was to be sure that the speech was printed precisely the way he had spoken it.

Lincoln always felt the freedom to depart from his notes or manuscript as he gave the speech. He spontaneously inserted "under God" into the Gettysburg Address.

Lincoln knew well the marks of a rhetorical culture. Conversation is two-way. The "real" audience to a speech talks back. An "ideal" audience does not speak back. Some modern editions of the Lincoln-Douglas debates have edited out comments from the audience, but to do so is to miss a high point of oral communication. In Lincoln's one-hour presentations or in his one-and-a-half-hour rebuttals, he did not do all the talking. The artful oral communicator always had to contend with the questions and opinions of the real audience.

Many cultural historians have fastened upon the phrase "the golden age of oratory" in attempting to capture the high commitment to rhetoric in nineteenth-century America. Edward Griffin Parker used this description in a book of that title in 1857. Parker, a lawyer and a member of the Massachusetts Senate, had in 1857 become the editor of the political department of the *Boston Traveler*. For Parker the hundred years began in 1760. He linked superb oratory with great causes and dated the beginning of this golden age with the rise of colonial statesmen bold enough to envision a new nation. "The capital of the orator is in the bank of the highest sentimentalities and the purest enthusiasms."[12] Publishing his book one year before the Lincoln-Douglas debates, Parker included no mention of the rail-splitter orator.

Although later writers have used the description of a "golden age" as wholly affirmative, Parker's book is more complex. His analysis is as much a lament to an age fast disappearing. Writing at mid-century, he deplored the present reality that "the age of heroes is over, and the age for their statues has come. The jubilant age of the Republic is drawing to a close." What are we left with? "A brazen age, antisentimental succeeds; an age, when sordid, calculating interest, rather than conscious merit dares to run after renown."[13] Parker suggested that the demise of oratory aids and abets this larger cultural demise.

Most intriguing is Parker's suggestion as to a major cause for the decline of oratory: reading. "The eyes in a measure supercede the ears." Why was reading the culprit? "The press carries the day against forum, tribune, and government." Parker's analysis, in comparing reading with speaking, was more than simply the view of an old fogy. The reality of change in antebellum America from a society of small, independent communities to a mass society was that a thousand people might hear the orator but tens of thousands would read the speech. The result might be a split verdict: "If the speech reads well, the verdict of the readers altogether out-votes those of the hearers."[14]

Parker anticipated the work of later rhetorical criticism when he observed that the shift from the spoken to the written word was "shifting the real for the ideal." In the spoken word, the speaker must at every moment be conscious of a specific audience. One of Lincoln's strengths as a speaker was his ability to adjust and amend his remarks in response to the questions and concerns expressed by a live audience. In the written word, the real audience becomes an ideal audience. This audience does not ask questions and does not speak back.

According to Parker, the best example of reading's having achieved priority over speaking was the changed practices in Congress. He described the new phenomenon of his day whereby a congressman read from notes "to a few unattentive colleagues, a learned and elaborate composition, which he chooses to call a 'speech.'" Parker protested: "The energy he should have thrown into its delivery, he expends in attending to its handsome publication. His constituency, who have read with delight his speech, to which nobody listened with attention, receive him upon his return with trumpets, and invite him to dinner." Parker observed that all of this new emphasis on the written instead of the spoken word worked to "bar" the "personal magnetism" of effective orators.[15]

Parker's remarks can serve to frame the rhetorical landscape in which Lincoln refined his oratory. Lincoln worked hard to learn the dynamics of the spoken word. He had to overcome his own physical appearance to win the right to be heard. His personal magnetism came to life through the ear, not the eye.

For many in the throng that day, expectations were shaped by memories of Lincoln's First Inaugural Address. Lincoln crafted that speech in the winter of 1860–61 in Springfield. He began his research in November 1860 by checking out of the Sangamon County Library in Springfield speeches of Daniel Webster and John C. Calhoun as well as earlier inaugural addresses. As he wrote and rewrote, Lincoln was somewhat removed from the crosscurrents of opinion swirling around in the nation's capital. How different would be the setting in wartime Washington in which he would write his Second Inaugural Address in the winter of 1865.

In his First Inaugural Address, Lincoln was intellectual and studied in tone. He reviewed the nature of the perpetuity of the government and contrasted it with an association of states. He spoke throughout of constitutional rights and responsibilities. He marshaled evidence to support his position as a lawyer arguing a case. He spoke as if he believed that he could achieve his objectives by rational argument.

Lincoln cast the responsibility for breaking up the Union on the Southern states. In the next-to-last paragraph he summarized his position.

> In *your* hands, my dissatisfied fellow countrymen, and not in mine, is the momentous issue of civil war. The government will not assail *you*. You can have no conflict, without being yourselves the aggressors. *You* have no oath registered to Heaven to destroy the government, while *I* shall have the most solemn one to "preserve, protect and defend" it.[16]

The last sentence may be balanced structurally, but in this case Lincoln's Southern listeners could not hear a rational, balanced argument.

What has been remembered most often from the First Inaugural are words from the final paragraph. In an abrupt
change of tone, Lincoln reached toward the emotions as well
as the intellect. "We are not enemies, but friends. We must
not be enemies."[17] For the audience, these words of healing
and unity must have sounded very different from what had
gone before. How these words came to be included opens another window on Lincoln's rhetorical practice.

Lincoln sought advice from friends and colleagues for the
First Inaugural. Before Lincoln left Springfield on February
11, Judge David Davis read the initial draft and agreed with
the entire speech. Fellow Illinois lawyer and Senator-Elect
Orville H. Browning, who accompanied Lincoln on the long
train trip east, was given a copy in Indianapolis. Browning
made a single but important suggestion. He argued that Lincoln should say nothing about retaking government property.
Francis P. Blair, Sr., read the speech in Washington and en-
thusiastically commended the whole address.

Lincoln arrived in Washington early on Saturday morning,
February 23, 1861. He and his family took quarters at
Willard's Hotel. During that first day, Lincoln gave a copy of
the address to William H. Seward, who was to be the secretary of state. Seward, formerly a senator from New York,
had led Lincoln on the first ballot for the Republican nomination for president. Lincoln genuinely respected Seward's
abilities and at first deferred to his experience. Seward read
the address, and by the next evening he had sent the president-elect a six-page letter with his suggestions.

Seward told Lincoln, "Your case is quite like that of Jefferson." Inaugurated in 1801, with the anger of the Federalists
almost visible in the air, Jefferson, as Seward reminded Lincoln, "sank the partisan in the patriot in his inaugural address, and propitiated his adversaries by declaring: 'We are

all Federalists, all Republicans.'" Seward concluded, "Be sure that while all your administrative conduct will be in harmony with Republican principles and policy, you cannot lose the Republican party by practicing in your advent to office the magnanimity of a victor."[18]

At the top of his six pages of suggestions, Seward offered two suggestions under the heading "General Remarks." After praising Lincoln's argument as "strong and conclusive," he told the president-elect that something additional was needed "to meet and remove prejudice and passion in the South, and despondency and fear in the East." What was needed? "Some words of affection—some of calm and cheerful confidence."[19]

Seward, who had achieved a reputation as an excellent public speaker, weighed in with no fewer than forty-nine suggestions. Lincoln received them graciously and incorporated twenty-seven of them in editing and rewriting.[20]

The most important changes were in the concluding paragraph, which addressed itself to "my dissatisfied fellow-countrymen." Lincoln's last sentence in his first draft was, "With you and not with me is the solemn question, Shall it be peace or a sword?" Seward proposed striking this ending. In its place he sent Lincoln two drafts of a new closing paragraph to substitute for the two sentences. The first paragraph, containing 139 words, was made up of both commonplace and sonorous phrases. The second paragraph, containing eighty-three words, contained the basis for a more poetic ending. Lincoln chose this second paragraph and gave to it even more life and beauty.

———

We can see Lincoln's sense of rhetoric at work by comparing sentences in the final paragraph, each reworked by Lincoln.

SEWARD	LINCOLN
I close.	I am loath to close.
We are not, we must not be, aliens or enemies, but fellow-countrymen and brethren.	We are not enemies, but friends. We must not be enemies.
Although passion has strained our bonds of affection too hardly, they must not, I am sure they will not, be broken.	Though passion may have strained, it must not break our bonds of affection.
The mystic chords which, proceeding from so many battlefields and so many patriot graves, pass through all the hearts and all the hearths in this broad continent of ours, will yet again harmonize in their ancient music when breathed upon by the guardian angel of the nation.	The mystic chords of memory, stretching from every battlefield, and patriot grave, to every living heart and hearth-stone, all over this broad land, will yet swell the chorus of the Union, when again touched, as surely they will be, by the better angels of our nature.

We can see Lincoln's pen at work in comparing his fourth sentence, "Though passion may have strained, it must not break our bonds of affection" with Seward's original suggestion. In four of the five sentences in the final paragraph, Lincoln reduced Seward's words.

We need to be clear about what we are not saying. The opposite of verbose is not simple. Lincoln was not bent on brevity alone. He was intent on precision. Sometimes precision might mean more. Observe that he took Seward's opening sentence of two words, "I close," and extended it to a sentence of five words, "I am loath to close." The extension in this case is an extension of the emotion of language that Lincoln wanted to achieve.

Lincoln also removed redundant words. Thus, Seward's "aliens or enemies" became in Lincoln's edited text "enemies"; "fellow-countrymen and brethren" became "friends." Seward's "pass through all the hearts and all the hearths in this broad continent of ours" became "to every living heart and hearth-stone, all over this broad land."

Moreover, the positive cumulative effect is to bring together words of assonance and alliteration. Assonance brings close together words or syllables with resemblance of sound. The effect of expanding Seward's first sentence to Lincoln's "I am loath to close" is to achieve a pleasing assonance in bringing together "loath" and "close." Alliteration, the repetition of initial consonant sounds in two or more neighboring words, is achieved by using the consonant "b" five times in the last two sentences of the address:

> *break*
>   *bonds*
>   *battlefield*
>   *broad*
>   *better*

We linger over the First Inaugural because we can experience Lincoln's rhetorical artistry line by line. Lincoln crafted his speech using the suggestions of others. He added nine alterations of his own to the original draft. His ultimate aim was to state that the Union would be preserved regardless of resistance. The suggestions, especially Seward's, softened the rhetoric. The words were Lincoln's. We see a master of phrase and words at work.[21]

"And the war came." The second paragraph of the Second Inaugural concludes with an astounding sentence. Four words. Four syllables. So much is suggested in so little.

In this brief, understated sentence, Lincoln acknowledged that *"the war came"* in spite of the best intentions of the political leaders of the land. *"And the war came"* in spite of the determination of the president himself.

The way Lincoln crafted this sentence suggests that when *"the war came,"* it took its own course. Great generals may believe they were managing war, but human agency alone does not decide the outcome or even the character of the war. As Lincoln looked back from the perspective of four long years, he saw that, all along, the war had had a life of its own.

Charles Royster, in *The Destructive War,* offers an insight that helps illuminate the meaning of the central image of *"war"* in this paragraph. He sets out to probe "the scale of destruction to which the participants committed themselves" in the Civil War. Royster observes, "Americans surprised themselves with the extent of violence they could attain."[22]

Lincoln, by 1862, was growing increasingly troubled that Americans did not really know "the causes or consequences of their own acts." Royster guides us through four years of escalating violence, focused especially on the actions of Sherman. In American memory, Sherman is both hero and, at the same time, the perpetrator of a style of warfare unleashed on civilians that had never been seen before in the United States.

Lincoln came to believe that "the participants had battled in confusion." The rational Lincoln, who found himself for four years at the eye of the storm, realized that reason could not explain the bloodshed and violence. The war, as a "work of human minds and deeds, had grown incomprehensible."[23]

Lincoln is setting the stage for a different angle of vision, an alternative perspective on the meaning of the war.

This sentence is both a transition and a foreshadowing. The audience doesn't know it yet, but *"And the war came"* will lift the conflict beyond mere human instrumentality. It suggests that no mortal being can control the fortunes of war. Lincoln wants his listeners to understand that this war cannot be understood simply as the fulfillment of human plans.

———

Undergirding his narration of events is a rhetorical artistry that gives this complex paragraph rhythm and movement. An inclusive motif resonant in the use of *"all,"* *"all,"* and *"both"* is the leading edge of a theme that will grow throughout the address. In this second paragraph, the word *"war"* pulsates in every sentence. Nine times in ninety-nine words the image of war is present. Finally, in the four-word last sentence, Lincoln shifts the sentence construction: *"And the war came."* War becomes the subject and is no longer a direct object of the actions of others. War has a life of its own, independent of presidents, generals, and soldiers.

How did Lincoln speak that final sentence: *"And the war came"*? Correspondent Brooks reported that there was applause at the sentence, *"Both parties deprecated war; but one of them would make war rather than let the nation survive; and the other would accept war rather than let it perish."* The cheers continued, producing a "considerable pause." Brooks went on to write of Lincoln, "He added sententiously *'and the war came.'"*[24]

"Sententiously." The *Oxford English Dictionary* gives the definition of this adverb as "tersely and pithily." The adjective, "sententious," is defined as "full of meaning" or "full of intelligence and wisdom."

But if Brooks can report the "what" of the meaning, he cannot tell us the *"how"* of the speaking. How did Lincoln say, *"And the war came"*? Did he say it loudly, as the culmination of the crescendo? This is possible. But I think not. I believe he spoke it softly, mournfully. *"And the war came."*

4

"... somehow, the cause
of the war ..."

The third paragraph begins:

One eighth of the whole population were colored slaves, not distributed generally over the Union, but localized in the Southern part of it. These slaves constituted a peculiar and powerful interest. All knew that this interest was, somehow, the cause of the war. To strengthen, perpetuate, and extend this interest was the object for which the insurgents would rend the Union, even by war; while the government claimed no right to do more than to restrict the territorial enlargement of it. Neither party expected for the war, the magnitude, or the duration, which it has already attained. Neither anticipated that the <u>cause</u> of the conflict might cease with, or even before, the conflict itself should cease. Each looked for an easier triumph, and a result less fundamental and astounding.

On March 26, 1864, Albert G. Hodges, editor of the Frankfort *Commonwealth* (Kentucky); Archibald Dixon, former senator from Kentucky; and Governor Thomas E. Bramlette called on Lincoln at the Executive Mansion. They came to express their concern about the dissatisfaction in their state over the enlistment of slaves as soldiers. Lincoln asked his fellow Kentuckians if he could make "a little speech" about why he felt obligated to change from his inaugural promise not to interfere with slavery to his course of action leading to the Emancipation Proclamation.

The three leaders were evidently persuaded by Lincoln's explanation. At the end of the meeting, Hodges asked if he could have a copy of the president's speech to take with him to Kentucky. Lincoln replied that what he had said was extemporaneous and not written. Lincoln told them to go home, and he would write a letter committing to paper what he had said to them.[1]

———

On April 4, 1864, nine days later, Lincoln wrote his promised letter (see appendix II). He knew it was important that these prominent citizens in a key border state understand both the vision and the restraints that had guided him. Lincoln recounted how, early in the war, he rebuffed attempts either to emancipate or to arm the slaves in the South. He reminded them that he had made successive appeals, especially to the border states, for compensated emancipation. Those appeals fell on deaf ears. Finally, he was "driven to the alternative of either surrendering the Union, and with it, the Constitution," or of arming Southern slaves. Lincoln admitted his ambivalence in that decision: "I hoped for greater gain than loss; but of this, I was not entirely confident."[2]

Lincoln's letter to Hodges, eleven months before the Second Inaugural Address, contains both logic and language that would reappear on March 4, 1865. The antecedents to the Second Inaugural Address are to be found in letters, interviews, and private musings rather than in previous public speeches. Some of this material did not become known until after Lincoln's death. Some big ideas contained in this "little speech" would later find their way into the opening sentences of the third paragraph of the Second Inaugural.

Hodges, Dixon, and Bramlette left their interview with Lincoln believing that they had been heard. Like many others who entered Lincoln's office, they went in with their own questions and concerns, not certain they could agree with this tall, awkward president. They left persuaded that they could trust Lincoln about a very difficult and complex issue in their home state.

————

What made Lincoln so persuasive? Aristotle defined rhetoric as the art of persuasion: "Let us define rhetoric to be a faculty of considering all the possible means of persuasion on every subject." If medicine "conduces to health and sickness," and arithmetic to numbers, then rhetoric is "able to consider the means of persuasion on *any* given subject whatsoever."[3]

The Greek philosopher laid the foundation for all subsequent discussions of the nature and uses of rhetoric. Aristotle counseled the Greeks in his *Treatise on Rhetoric* that the means of persuasion must include both intrinsic and extrinsic proofs.

By extrinsic proof Aristotle meant direct evidence that was not the creation of the speaker's art. Direct evidence could include laws, contracts, and oaths, as well as the testimony of witnesses. In the legal proceedings of Aristotle's time, this kind of evidence was usually obtained in advance, recorded, put in sealed urns, and read in court.[4]

Intrinsic proof was that created by the art of the orator. Aristotle distinguished three kinds of intrinsic proof: (1) originating in the character of the speaker; (2) resident in the mind of the audience; and (3) inherent in the form and phrase of the speech itself. Rhetoric is a form of persuasion that is to be approached from these three directions and in that order.

Aristotle argued that *ethos* (ηθος), or credibility, was the most powerful means of persuasion. He listed the three most important qualities as character, intelligence, and good will. When the speaker exhibits those characteristics, "he will have the confidence of his hearers."[5]

In the Greek system of law, it was customary for a person to plead his own case. In this setting, *ethos* became extremely important. The speaker would want to weave into the speech elements that would speak to his character. He could also introduce witnesses who could testify to his integrity. But the primary use of rhetoric was in the plane of politics. The way we first judge the politician is by consciously or unconsciously taking the measure of his integrity.

Although it is unlikely that Lincoln had read Aristotle, I suggest that Lincoln understood intuitively the basic principles of the *Treatise on Rhetoric*. He embodied the Greek philosopher's definition of *ethos*. The audience quickly discerned that Lincoln was not playing a political role when he addressed them.

Phillips Brooks, the remarkable nineteenth-century Episcopal minister, who would speak so often about Lincoln during the time of mourning after his death, defined preaching in his Lyman Beecher Lectures at Yale as "truth through personality."[6] When Lincoln spoke, those who had not heard him before were sometimes put off at first by his appearance. Often he began his speeches in a tenor, almost falsetto voice that friends say was the product of nervousness. But quickly, usually within the first minutes, his voice deepened, and he conveyed the truth of his message in part because of the integrity of his person.

As people listened to Lincoln speak, they learned to trust him. Obviously, trust could be won more directly in the face-to-face encounters of rural or small-town Illinois. When Lincoln entered the national stage as president in 1861, this trust was harder to win. At Gettysburg, and now again at his Second Inaugural, Lincoln's credibility undergirded and reinforced the content of his message.

The greater the difficulty of the message, the more important that the bond of trust be established between the speaker and the audience. I am certain that Lincoln understood, as he began the critical third paragraph of his address, that the surprising and difficult words that lay ahead would only be heard if he won the right to be heard.

———

Aristotle's second type of *ethos* is the speaker's ability to move the audience. This, the psychological element in rhetoric, depends on the ability of the speaker to discern the state of mind or psychological mood of the audience.

How does this second characteristic of *ethos* work in rhetorical practice? The speaker needs to understand the audience. What expectations does it bring? What information does the audience know or need to know? What impediments might block effective communication?

How did Lincoln understand his audience on that blustery March Saturday? He knew that these inaugural spectators included everyone from government employees to supporters who had traveled long distances to be present. Soldiers from the many area hospitals made up a sizable portion of the assembly. And Lincoln understood that the audience would ultimately include the nation, as the public read his address in the days and weeks to come.

I believe that Lincoln discerned the mood of his audience as anxious. He had encountered this frame of mind in many interviews. Underneath the ebullience at the realization that the war was finally drawing to a close lay many questions about the uncertain peace. This long war, which continually erupted in tragedy and loss, produced an anxiety about the future. Even as plans were being debated for reconstruction, most knew that important members of Lincoln's own party disagreed with his policies for the restoration of the Southern states.

Impatience also lay in waiting. His hearers were impatient about the many false signs that an end to the killing and destruction was near. The war effort had united factions in the North, but it had also exposed fissures in the political foundations of the nation. Lincoln was deeply concerned that a nation divided in war would remain a nation divided in peace. Would the American people have enough patience for a peace process that he knew would take far longer than the four years of war? Speaking to an audience whose emotions had been whipsawed during four turbulent years, Lincoln sought to allay their anxiety and impatience.

———

Lincoln put his credibility on the line as he began the central paragraph, in which he would advance from historical to political to theological explanation. This paragraph contains 394 of the 703 words of the address.

Lincoln shifted from chronicler to persuader. Although he still refrained from "I," we begin to feel his personal intensity. The last four sentences of the second paragraph and the initial seven sentences of paragraph three refer to the past.

> *All dreaded it—all sought to avert it. While the inaugeral {sic} address was being delivered from this place, devoted altogether to* saving *the Union without war . . . seeking to dissole {sic} the Union, and divide effects, by negotiation. Both parties deprecated war; but one of them would* make *war rather than let the nation survive; and the other would* accept *war rather than let it perish. And the war came.*

> *One eighth of the whole population were colored slaves, not distributed generally over the Union, but localized in the Southern part of it. These slaves constituted a peculiar and powerful interest. All knew that this interest was, somehow, the cause of the war. To strengthen, perpetuate, and extend this interest was the object for which the insurgents would rend the Union, even*

by war; while the government claimed no right to do more than to restrict the territorial enlargement of it. Neither party expected for the war, the magnitude, or the duration, which it has already attained. Neither anticipated that the <u>cause</u> of the conflict might cease with, or even before, the conflict itself should cease. Each looked for an easier triumph, and a result less fundamental and astounding.

Now the balance of paragraph three and the entire concluding paragraph would focus on the present and the future. Speaking to an audience that he believed was filled with anxiety and impatience, Lincoln the lawyer-politician was about to plead a difficult case.

The intensity rose when, in the third sentence, Lincoln stated that slavery was *"somehow"* the cause of the war. *"Somehow"* is the key that holds these initial sentences of the paragraph in balance. The *"somehow"* qualifies the assertion that *"all knew"* that slavery was the cause of the war. In and under the adverb *"somehow,"* Lincoln hinted at his own brooding and painful journey to grasp the true meaning of the war.

Lincoln structured this paragraph so that it built in a crescendo of anticipation. His use of parallel structures,

Neither party expected . . . Neither anticipated . . .

reinforced the message of the previous paragraph. In the end, both sides had shared values and attitudes.

Lincoln knew, even though the audience did not yet know, that he was about to forge new ground for an inaugural address. As he readied himself to move beyond temporal markers to timeless markers, he must surely have asked himself if he could carry his audience with him. He must have known he was taking a risk.

Lincoln approached the *"somewhat"* of American slavery from several directions in this third paragraph. He started with description, moved to analysis, and then—suddenly, un-expectedly—became sermonic. Four times in this paragraph, Lincoln would quote from the Bible. And there are echoes of other Biblical texts, references that many in his audience that day surely heard and understood.

In this paragraph, we experience Lincoln's use of both rea-son and emotion. The opening sentences are a closely rea-soned argument about the historical causation of the war. Suddenly the language changes. We experience a deeper emo-tion in Lincoln's words. We recall that the impetus for his emotional language at the conclusion of the First Inaugural grew out of Secretary of State Seward's suggestions. Here, in the Second Inaugural, Lincoln abruptly changed to emo-tional language that was entirely of his own construction.

In the first sentence, he described the extent and location of slavery: these slaves were not *"distributed generally"* but were *"localized."* Here we encounter the first of Lincoln's three changes to the text of the Second Inaugural. In the last clause of the sentence (see appendix I), the word *"part"* replaces the original word "half." We do not know why he made this change, but I suggest it was because the original word "half" might imply that slavery had equal territorial standing. The clause, *"the Southern part of it,"* underscored the reality that slavery was located only in the South, and therefore occupied far less than half of the territory of the United States.

In the second sentence, Lincoln added analysis. He moved from a description of geography to more analytical language about economics. Lincoln chose his terms carefully. *"These slaves constituted"* both *"a peculiar"* and a *"powerful interest."*

Slavery had long been called a "peculiar institution" in the South. It became increasingly peculiar in the nineteenth cen-tury, as white Southerners found themselves more and more defensive and isolated. There were several peculiarities in their situation. First, the old argument, that some of the ancestors of Southern blacks had been slaves in Africa, seemed over time to have become immaterial. Second, their owners had justified holding slaves because blacks had been "heathens" in Africa. This argument didn't hold up, because by now so many had become Christians. Third, the Declaration of Independence enunciated the Enlightenment doctrine of natural rights and the dignity of all persons. The South's greatest statesman, Thomas Jefferson, had championed this viewpoint. Finally, by the middle of the century, outside of Africa, only Brazil, Cuba, Dutch Guiana, and Puerto Rico remained as societies with masters and slaves.[7]

By using the term *"powerful interest,"* Lincoln points to the economic interest represented in slavery. An adroit student of political economy, Lincoln understood the South's economic dependence on cotton and slavery.

Gabor S. Boritt has shown that before 1854 economic motifs were central in Lincoln's political thinking. If after 1854 slavery became the critical subject in Lincoln's speeches, we should not miss the economic component in his thought. Lincoln's economic purpose for America was the right of every person to rise. Slavery threatened this American dream. "By denying blacks the right to rise, slavery endangered that right for all."[8]

Less than thirty years later, a son of the South, Woodrow Wilson, wrote about the economics of slavery. Wilson, a young professor of jurisprudence and political economy at Princeton College, had been invited by Albert Bushnell Hart of Harvard University to write the third volume in the *Epochs of American History* series. In *Division and Reunion: 1829–1889,* published in 1893, Wilson chronicled the political economy that emerged in the South. With Eli Whitney's invention of the cotton gin in 1793, cotton production be-

came enormously more profitable in the early nineteenth century. After tracing the amazing growth of this staple product,
Wilson observed, "Slavery seemed nothing less than the indispensable economic instrument of southern society."[9]

In the crucial third sentence of this third paragraph, Lincoln brought together all persons, all parties, all interests. After two-thirds of a century of debate, and four years of war,
during which slavery was the central reason for disagree-
ment, Lincoln now stated, *"All knew that this interest was,
somehow, the cause of the war."*

In placement, this sentence is the geographical and literary
center of Lincoln's Second Inaugural. Rather than listing all the
reasons the two sides had advanced for the war, from protect-
ing states' rights to preserving the Union, Lincoln simply said,
"All knew." They knew, whether they would admit it or not.

This sentence also represents just how far Lincoln had
come in his understanding of the cause and purpose of the
war. Here Lincoln inverted the priorities of the war. If, at the
beginning of the war, the emphasis was continually on preserving the Union, by the end of the war, at the Second Inaugural, the focus was on securing liberty for all. For Lincoln,
preserving the Union and emancipating the slaves was always
a two-step. The second step had come second in the chronology of the war, but now, *"somehow,"* it had become primary.

As Lincoln began his discussion of slavery, the colors in his
language were muted. *"Interest"* and *"cause"* are words with
subdued coloring. Lincoln, superintending a civil war, deliberately chose to reduce the intensity of his words in discussing a volatile subject.[10]

One gains an appreciation for the muted tones of Lincoln's
words by comparing his rhetoric on slavery with the words of

two of his contemporaries, William Lloyd Garrison and Harriet Beecher Stowe. Garrison, the leading abolitionist of the era, founded *The Liberator* on January 1, 1831. He started the American Anti-Slavery Society in 1833. The tactic of Garrison and many of his fellow abolitionists was to employ an emotional rhetoric to provoke and assail. In the first issue of *The Liberator*, Garrison stated: "I am in earnest—I will not equivocate—I will not excuse—I will not retreat a single inch—and I will be heard." Garrison's rhetoric is what today we would call "in your face." All the rhetoric begins with "I."

In the early 1830s, Garrison came to believe that the Constitution was a proslavery document that had only been ratified by giving in to the South on the issue of slavery. He attacked the Constitution. "A sacred compact, forsooth! We pronounce it the most blood and heaven-daring arrangement ever made for the continuance and protection of a system of the most atrocious villainy ever exhibited on earth."[11] Garrison burned the Constitution in public.

By 1842, Garrison was advocating disunion. At the annual meeting of the Massachusetts Anti-slavery Society in 1843, he aimed his fiery rhetoric at the relationship between the North and the South. "The compact which exists between the North and the South is a 'covenant with death, and an agreement with hell'—involving both parties in atrocious criminality; and should be immediately annulled."[12]

Lincoln believed that Garrison's style of rhetoric alienated the uncommitted. In every speech after 1854 Lincoln spoke against slavery, but at the same time he felt committed to and restrained by the Constitution. In the 1840s, the abolitionists had turned their rhetoric against each other as they divided over a number of issues, including the role of moral suasion versus political action and the place of women in the abolitionist movement. Although toward the end of the Civil War

Lincoln expressed his appreciation for Garrison's courage, his quarrel with the abolitionists was that their rhetoric inflamed and thus polarized the public.

———

As sectional animosities were increasing in the 1850s, a New England housewife dramatized the evils of slavery with a story that reached an audience beyond the words of any politician or abolitionist. Harriet Beecher Stowe's *Uncle Tom's Cabin* was published in March 1852 and quickly became the publishing marvel of the century. With eight power presses running twenty-four hours a day in Boston, sales of the book roared past three hundred thousand copies by the end of the year.

Stowe was a member of one of the nineteenth century's most famous families. Her father, Lyman Beecher, and her brothers Edward and Henry Ward Beecher were prominent ministers, educators, and reformers. Her sister Catharine was a well-known educator and feminist leader. "Hattie," at home with her children in Brunswick, Maine, found time to write a novel that grew to forty-five chapters with at least as many characters.

The central character is Uncle Tom. The term "Uncle Tom" took on negative associations in the twentieth century. Modern readers are generally surprised when they read Stowe's novel and discover the original Uncle Tom. Her portrait of Uncle Tom is of a Christ-figure, a resilient man of unlimited goodness with a love for all people. In the person of Tom, Stowe showed that Christian character is often more resident in blacks than in whites.

Her language was romantic; her words overflowed with pathos. Today we might say that Stowe overwrote. She described the blacks as "bound and bleeding at the foot of civilized and Christianized humanity, imploring compassion in vain." In the final chapter, Stowe told her readers that what they had read was not fiction. In the language of a crusader, she said that "there are living witnesses all over our land to testify" to parallels to Uncle Tom and other characters in her novel. She asserted that America owed the African race reparations for the wrongs committed. At the end of the novel, she appealed to the people of the South: "Have you not, in your own secret souls, in your own private conversings, felt that there are woes and evils, in this accursed system?"[13]

Stowe had been lukewarm in her support of Lincoln in the election of 1860, and she quickly became disappointed with the new president. She complained about Lincoln's First Inaugural by asking the question first asked by Sojourner Truth, "Is God dead?"[14] Stowe was furious with Lincoln when he overrode General John C. Frémont's 1861 initiative to liberate slaves in Missouri.[15]

In November 1862, Stowe traveled to Washington to see if she could encourage the talk about an Emancipation Proclamation to become a reality. Stowe called upon the president at the White House on a cold November evening. She was accompanied by Henry Wilson, senator from Massachusetts, and her twelve-year-old son, Charley. A family story has it that as Mrs. Stowe entered the room Lincoln greeted her with the words, "So you are the little woman who made this great war."[16]

Within a year, Stowe's growing appreciation for Lincoln came forward in an article published in *The Watchman and Reflector* and reprinted in *Littell's Living Age*. Having met Lincoln, and now following his actions and words more closely, she saw a side to "Father Abraham" that had eluded her. "Lincoln is a strong man," she wrote, "but his strength is of a peculiar kind; it is not aggressive so much as passive." What did she mean? She answered, "It is like the strength not so much of a stone buttress as of a wire cable." After watching Lincoln now for nearly three years, Stowe said, "It is a strength swaying to every influence, yielding on this side and on that to popular needs, yet tenaciously and inflexibly bound to carry its great end."[17] Unyielding in her own opposition to slavery, Stowe offered an appreciation of the flexible strength of a president contending in the world of politics.

The colors of Lincoln's rhetoric on slavery are muted compared with the styles of Garrison and Stowe. Whereas the latter two focused on the South, Lincoln had always focused on the extension of slavery into the territories. Garrison and Stowe were uncompromising in their attitude toward the South; Lincoln's words were more tolerant. Garrison and Stowe talked and wrote about the atrocities associated with slavery; Lincoln was convinced that slavery was a moral evil, but as president he chose not to speak about slavery in overly emotional language. Garrison attacked the slave owners; Lincoln almost never did. Stowe's and Garrison's words were able to arouse powerful emotions; Lincoln's words were less dramatic, but also less frightening. When Lincoln became president of all the people, he most often chose to speak in language that he believed would not ignite, and just might convince the uncommitted.

———

Standing behind many great speeches are ideas that are not articulated in the actual words of an address. Standing behind the Second Inaugural Address is Lincoln's fidelity to the Constitution. The word "Constitution" is never used in the address, but the nature and meaning of the Constitution are present throughout. Fidelity to the Constitution, when it came to the issue of slavery, worked to restrain the actions of the president.

The closest the Constitution came to breaking through to the text of the address is when Lincoln said, *"The government claimed no right to do more than to restrict the territo-*

rial enlargement of" slavery. The "*more*" in the above sentence is the Southern states' fear that the government would interfere in the then established institution of slavery.

Lincoln addressed that fear early in his First Inaugural Address, when he said, "I have no purpose, directly or indirectly, to interfere with the institution of slavery in the States where it exists. I believe I have no legal right to do so, and I have no inclination to do so."[18] Lincoln took the unusual tack for an inaugural address of quoting words from a previous speech. He did so, I believe, to indicate that he had always been restrained by the Constitution, not that he was now announcing some new strategy aimed at assuaging recent Southern complaints. He hoped that this assurance would allay fears in the South that he and the federal government would attempt to interfere with the peculiar institution so deeply entrenched in the South.

Lincoln's challenge as president was how to balance his opposition to slavery and his fidelity to the Constitution. He was aware that there was a certain truth in Garrison's charge that the Constitution was a compromise document that allowed slavery in the South. Lincoln had, however, argued at Cooper Union in 1860 that the founders were united in opposing the spread of slavery to the new territories. He came to believe that the founders believed or hoped that slavery would one day become extinct.

————

The letter to Hodges in the spring of 1864 is one of the best examples of the tension that Lincoln felt between being against slavery and for the Constitution. The first words of his "little speech" were: "I am naturally anti-slavery. If slavery is not wrong, nothing is wrong. I can not remember when I did not so think, and feel." The words are unequivocal. Lincoln followed them with, "And yet I have never understood that the Presidency conferred upon me an unrestricted right to act officially upon this judgment and feeling." Why? His dilemma was in the oath he took to "defend the Constitution of the United States." He expressed the problem and the possibility in a most Lincolnesque statement: "I could not take the office without taking the oath."[19]

One may criticize Lincoln for his attitudes on race, or the timing of emancipation, but only if there is a prior acknowledgment of the centrality of the Constitution in both his political and moral thinking. The integrity of this fidelity to the Constitution shines through in sentence after sentence of this private letter. Thus, "I understood, too, that in ordinary civil administration this oath even forbade me to practically indulge my primary abstract judgment on the moral question of slavery."[20]

In the spring of 1864, Lincoln's remarks about slavery and the Constitution were meant to assure these three leaders from a border state that, whatever his personal convictions, he had never acted precipitously. He shared his own convictions, but he was at pains to emphasize the restraints he felt as one that had taken an oath "that I would, to the best of my ability, preserve, protect, and defend the Constitution of the United States."[21]

Lincoln decided to "add a word which was not in the verbal conversation" as the last paragraph of the letter to Hodges.

> In telling this tale I attempt no complement to my own sagacity. I claim not to have controlled events, but confess plainly that events have controlled me. Now, at the end of three years struggle the nation's condition is not what either party, or any man devised, or expected. God alone can claim it. Whither it is tending seems plain. If God now wills the removal of a great wrong, and wills also that we of the North as well as you of the South, shall pay fairly for our complicity in that

wrong, impartial history will find therein new cause to attest and revere the justice and goodness of God.[22]

An overarching theme of his "little speech" was historical causation. The final paragraph, which he had not expressed to Hodges, Dixon, and Bramlette in his office, offers several clues to Lincoln's understanding of the dilemma of historical cause and effect.

One idea in the letter to Hodges, which surfaces again in the Second Inaugural, is the different expectations of the various parties. In the letter Lincoln says, "Now, at the end of three years struggle the nation's condition is not what either party, or any man devised, or expected." This idea is expanded and reshaped in the Second Inaugural to read, *"Neither party expected for the war, the magnitude, or the duration, which it has already attained."* The key idea that links these two sentences is the expectations of the parties. The antecedent in the letter to Hodges is an indication of how long and how much Lincoln had thought about historical causation. The larger point is that all the parties were surprised by the turn of events.

––––––

The clues in the final paragraph of the letter to Hodges have been and can be read quite differently. David H. Donald, in his biography, *Lincoln,* chooses one line from this final paragraph as a clue or symbol for his entire biography. On the frontispiece of Donald's biography are Lincoln's words to Hodges: "I claim not to have controlled events, but confess plainly that events have controlled me." Donald goes on to say in his preface, "This biography highlights a basic trait of character evident throughout Lincoln's life: the essential passivity of his nature."[23]

One of the problems with Donald's choice of this sentence

is its selectivity. Obviously, Donald builds a case for the thesis of his biography from many sources, and not just this one sentence. The problem with highlighting the sentence from the letter to Hodges is that it neglects or distorts the whole of Lincoln's intention in the final paragraph of the letter.

The burden of the new paragraph is neither Lincoln's passivity nor even the surprise of the parties. The central meaning was Lincoln's assertion that God was the primary actor in this drama. Lincoln's acknowledgment of his own passivity is his way of pointing to the larger truth of the activity of God.

Lincoln's focus on God as actor is announced four times. First, after Lincoln spoke about the condition of the nation being "not what either party, or any man devised, or expected," he concluded, "God alone can claim it." Are Lincoln's thoughts about God here expressed in resignation or affirmation? We need to read on. In the second and third instances, Lincoln asserted that God was the supreme actor who "wills." God both "wills the removal of a great wrong," and "wills also that we of the North as well as you of the South, shall pay fairly for our complicity in that wrong." In the fourth instance, the reality that "the nation's condition is not what either party, or any man devised," is the ultimate reason why Lincoln concludes, "Impartial history will find therein new cause to attest and revere the justice and goodness of God." These attestations are not passive acquiescence but, rather, an avowal of God acting in history.

We will discuss Lincoln's understanding of God's judgment and goodness in much larger compass in chapter 6. We will see how this last paragraph of the Hodges letter is a seedbed for ideas that will be expressed in yet more dramatic language about *"American Slavery"* in the next sections of the Second Inaugural.

We have now reached the closing stages of a paradox that has been building sentence by sentence, paragraph by paragraph, in the first half of the speech. The question Lincoln was wrestling with was: who is responsible for this war?

In the opening paragraph, Lincoln began building this paradox, although the audience barely recognized its initial building blocks. In the second paragraph, Lincoln built the tension in the paradox by comparing the aspirations of the *parties* in the crisis. On the one hand, Lincoln emphasized the unity of all sides in not wanting war. On the other hand, he set up the antithesis between those who would *make* war to break up the Union and those who would *accept* war to conserve it.

In the opening lines of this third paragraph, Lincoln argued that *"all knew"* that slavery *"was, somehow, the cause of the war."* The paradox was refocused in the antithesis that *"insurgents"* wanted *"to strengthen, perpetuate, and extend"* slavery, whereas *"the government"* only sought to *"restrict the territorial enlargement of it."*

The final plank in the paradox is that both parties expected victory. In fact, *"each looked for an easier triumph."* Neither was prepared, to turn Lincoln's negative into a positive, for a *"result"* so *"fundamental and astounding."*

Lincoln had now prepared his audience for the resolution of the paradox. Who was responsible for this war? He had led them to a pathway that offered no human resolution. He asserted that the results in the spring of 1865 were not what any of the leaders or parties could have imagined in 1861.

5

"Both read the same Bible, and pray to the same God . . ."

The third paragraph continues:

Both read the same Bible, and pray to the same God; and each invokes His aid against the other. It may seem strange that any men should dare to ask a just God's assistance in wringing their bread from the sweat of other men's faces; but let us judge not that we be not judged. The prayers of both could not be answered; that of neither has been answered fully.

When the decision was made to consecrate the ground at Gettysburg, a monumental task lay ahead. There were left behind more than fifty thousand Confederate and Union dead, wounded, or missing soldiers from the remarkable battle of July 1–3, 1863. About six thousand, half Union, lay on the battlefield. How were these soldiers to be buried before Edward Everett, Lincoln, and other dignitaries arrived for the dedication of the battlefield and cemetery in November?

Andrew Curtin, the Republican governor of Pennsylvania, appointed David Wills, a successful banker and civic leader of Gettysburg, to oversee plans for the cemetery and the dedication. One major assignment was to sort the possessions of the soldiers who lay there. Clothing was searched. Belongings were labeled and stored so that family members would be able to recover them—pocket diaries, letters, and photographs, as well as money, watches, and jewelry.

What chiefly survived were Bibles.[1] An overwhelming number of the soldiers, from North and South, carried Bibles. Most often the Bible was a pocket New Testament. *"Both read the same Bible."*

———

When Lincoln introduced the Bible into the Second Inaugural, we entered new territory in presidential inaugural addresses. Before Lincoln, there were eighteen inaugural addresses delivered by fourteen presidents.[2] From George Washington to Lincoln's predecessor, James Buchanan, each referred to God or the Deity. These references almost always came in the last paragraph. The mention of God or a Divine Being was in the form of the need for reliance on or guidance from the "Parent of the Human Race" (George Washington), the "Patron of Order" (John Adams), "Infinite Power" (Thomas Jefferson), "Almighty Being" (James Madison), "Almighty God" (James Monroe and Andrew Jackson), and "Divine Providence" (James Buchanan).[3]

The Bible was quoted only once in those eighteen addresses. John Quincy Adams, who consistently brought his Calvinist moral concerns to his long career in public service, was said to have read the Bible every day of his life. In his supplication for divine favor for himself and his country, Adams affirms the providence of God by quoting from the Psalms: "Except the Lord keep the city, the watchman waketh but in vain" (Psalm 127:1). The Biblical verse functions, like the references to God in all the other addresses, as a part of the need for reliance on God.[4] Adams's reference is in contrast to the way the Bible functions in Lincoln's Second Inaugural, but the lack of precedent did not deter Lincoln. In the 340 words remaining in the Second Inaugural, Lincoln would quote or paraphrase four Biblical passages.

The introduction of the Bible signaled Lincoln's determination to think theologically as well as politically about the war. *"Both read the same Bible, and pray to the same God"* is filled with multiple meaning. Lincoln was acknowledging the universal use of the Bible and prayer by soldiers throughout the war. Before we attempt to understand still other layers of meaning, we will pause to appreciate the use of the Bible that Lincoln describes and affirms.

With the beginning of hostilities, Bibles were produced almost as quickly as bullets. The American Bible Society made the decision to supply Bibles to all soldiers. At the Bible House, headquarters of the ABS in New York City, sixteen power presses printed and bound the books. The increase in the publication of Bibles was astonishing. In the first year of the Civil War, the American Bible Society printed 370,000 more Bibles than in the previous year.[5]

The American Bible Society was founded as a voluntary society in New York City in 1816. This national society was an amalgamation of more than one hundred Bible societies scattered in communities and states across the nation. The ABS rapidly became the flagship society of more than three hundred evangelical voluntary societies founded in the first decades of the nineteenth century. Although churches had been disestablished in the new nation, these benevolent societies constituted a new kind of Protestant Christian establishment. The evangelical voluntary societies were associations of individuals gathered together to do specific tasks. Laity, not clergy, directed them. The principle of voluntarism opened the door for participation by women. These associations of individuals, organized around tasks rather than creeds, also promoted cooperation across denominational lines.

Societies such as the American Tract Society, the American Education Society, the American Peace Society, the American Society for the Promotion of Temperance, and the American Anti-Slavery Society drew upon Congregationalists, Presbyterians, Episcopalians, Baptists, Methodists, and members of smaller denominations for common tasks. The American Tract Society cooperated closely with the ABS in providing materials for soldiers. Most of the societies operated as a kind of "Evangelical United Front," engaged in tasks in education, evangelism, mission, and reform in the decades before the Civil War. This united front, to use a term from political science, enabled individuals "to achieve ends far beyond the powers of their separate denominations."[6]

In a rapidly expanding nation, these voluntary societies became the advance guard for evangelism and reform. Orestes Brownson, an irascible reformer, captured the incredible reach of these societies. He observed, "Matters have come to such a pass, that a peaceable man can hardly venture to eat or drink, to go to bed or to get up, to correct his children or kiss his wife, without obtaining the permission and the direction of some moral . . . society."[7]

The centrality of the Bible in nineteenth-century America cannot be overemphasized. The publication of the Bible soared above all other books. Christians understood the Bible to be the Word of God. Ordinary citizens were confident in their ability to understand the Bible. If in the twentieth century people would argue over the authority and interpretation of the Bible, in the nineteenth the Bible was fundamentally a personal resource in life and in death. In the early decades of the century, in an exploding print culture, the challenge was to ensure that the Bible continued to be pre-eminent in the competition with many other books.[8]

If the Puritans had been known as "the people of the Book," the ABS wanted to disseminate the Book to an expanding and increasingly diverse America. In 1829, it announced its intention to provide "a Bible to every household" within two years. This strategy was called the "General Supply." The result would never match the intention, but the society mounted four such supplies in the nineteenth century.[9]

The American Bible Society went into action as the Civil War began. The first strategy was for agents, working through local auxiliaries, to supply the soldiers with Bibles when they enlisted. The Bible Society met the troops in their home villages or towns or where they gathered in state encampments before heading south. The New Hampshire Auxiliary Bible Society supplied eight regiments and individual companies with six thousand Bibles. The New York Bible Society supplied Bibles to soldiers who were passing through the city, and to the sailors on ships anchored in New York Harbor.

A second phase of the Bible Society's work was supplying troops directly in the field. The United States Christian Commission, formed in 1862, became the main distributor of American Bible Society Bibles during the war. Much of this effort became resupply, as Bibles were destroyed or left behind on wounded and dead soldiers. The Bibles in soldiers' kits or knapsacks might be "parched by drought, flooded by cloudburst, or become food for insects."[10]

The King James Version, completed in England in 1611, was the standard Bible in Lincoln's time. If the language was beautiful for Lincoln and his generation, it may sound stilted and strange to many ears today. What is sometimes forgotten is that this fresh translation in England was aimed at the common people of its day. Starting in the 1830s, there were attempts in the United States to update the language of the King James Version, but before the Civil War none of these efforts had been successful, because of the attachment of people to both the language and cadences of what they called the Authorized Version.

Catholics called the King James Version the Protestant

Bible. Therefore, starting in 1825, a number of editions of a Catholic Bible were published in the United States. The official Catholic Bible was the Douay Version, a vernacular translation in English, based on the Vulgate, a Latin version authorized by the Catholic church.[11]

It soon became clear that the soldiers would rather not be burdened with carrying the entire Bible. Most of the Bibles that would be produced were called pocket Bibles. They were in fact pocket New Testaments. Sometimes they included the Psalms. These Bibles were small and compact, usually measuring anywhere from 3¾ by 2½ to 4½ by 3¼ inches. A soldier could carry this pocket book on his person rather than in his luggage.

In 1863, the board of managers of the American Bible Society made a further concession to the exigencies of war. They decided to print still smaller portions of the Bible. The Psalms and Proverbs from the Old Testament were printed. Luke, John, Romans, 1 and 2 Corinthians, plus four other portions from the New Testament were printed to aid the mobile soldier. Looking back in 1866, ABS records revealed that it had published 5,297,832 Bibles in different formats.

The number of Bibles in the Civil War points to a larger phenomenon. James M. McPherson, in *For Cause and Comrades: Why Men Fought in the Civil War*, writes, "Civil War armies were, arguably, the most religious in American history." These soldiers were the products of the Second Great Awakening, a movement that erupted in episodes of both revival and reform in the first half of the century. After examining the letters and diaries of 1,076 soldiers, McPherson found that various religious practices, such as reading the Bible and prayer, "helped many soldiers overcome their fear of death." Many Bibles were inscribed with a verse of Scripture. John D. Pugh of Company B, 7th Regiment, Ohio, inscribed in his pocket New Testament, "seek an inheritance in that home where there is no parting."[12]

Alfred Kazin included an essay on Lincoln in his last book before his death. In *God and the American Writer,* Kazin assessed American writers' struggles to accept or deny God in their writings. In appraising Lincoln, Kazin writes of the centrality of the Bible for Lincoln and his culture. "The Bible was still an essential personal resource for this generation of Americans." The sacrifice of so many lives was to be explained not simply by patriotism but by the promise of salvation found in the Bible, that there is surely "a life beyond this one, a judgment superior to the earthly judgment." Kazin employs the analogy that the Bible therefore becomes the "bridge" in the Civil War between the temporal and the eternal. "The Bible was still a bridge between life and death."[13]

During the Civil War, soldiers on both sides offered eloquent testimony to the companionship of their pocket Bibles as an ally in their regular skirmishes with death. An unexpected byproduct of these pocket Bibles was their capacity for blocking death at the bridge between life and death. A bullet at the Battle of Manassas in July 1861 struck a lieutenant in the 6th North Carolina Regiment. He was carried to a field hospital, where he was pronounced mortally wounded. The doctor, upon closer examination, found that the bullet had struck the Bible in the lieutenant's breast pocket and thus saved him from instant death. Even though the soldier died, the story of protection by a "holy shield" circulated far and wide. The Confederate lieutenant was but the first of a number of soldiers who, it was said, were saved by their pocket Bibles.[14]

———

The ABS was a national society, but how would it distribute Bibles in the South after the fall of Fort Sumter in April 1861? Before the war, most of the Southern states had been at the forefront of support for the American Bible Society. Thomas J. "Stonewall" Jackson, while a Presbyterian professor in Virginia before the war, had long been a supporter of Bible printing and distribution. He went house to house to collect money for the work of the American Bible Society.

In the opening months of the war, the ABS put several strategies in place to supply Bibles across battle lines, despite a ban on all trade. At first Bibles were sent around the flanks of the armies that were gathering on both sides. Thus, Bibles from Baltimore, despite the long border between Maryland and Virginia, were sent to Virginia via the Chesapeake Bay and then on to the Auxiliary in Richmond at the very time that Northern newspapers took up the war cry "On to Richmond."

In the West, Bibles bound for General (and Episcopal Bishop) Leonidas Polk's Confederate army at Columbus, Kentucky, in early 1862 were at first stopped as contraband by federal troops at Cairo, Illinois. Finally, Commanders Ulysses S. Grant and Polk worked out a flag of truce for Bibles. Regular shipments of Bibles under such flags were sent south from New York via Fort Monroe and City Point. Secretary of War Stanton approved this measure, and the Norfolk Steamship Company paid all the shipping expenses. As late as December 1863, in response to a request from Levi Thorne, pastor of the Baptist church at Kingston, North Carolina, the American Bible Society approved a shipment of one hundred thousand volumes to North Carolina. This flag of truce for Bibles could only be worked out in a culture where "*both read the same Bible.*"

Before the end of the first year of hostilities, political loyalties severed the American Bible Society at the Mason-Dixon Line. The Southern auxiliaries broke off contact with the central office in New York. In Richmond, a former Southern auxiliary of the ABS began to print Bibles to be supplied to

Confederate soldiers. In March 1862, a convention in Augusta, Georgia, representing different societies in the South, organized the Bible Society of the Confederate States of America. This Confederate Bible Society also produced mainly pocket New Testaments. As the economic situation of the South worsened, most of the Bibles produced were reduced to paperboard covers.[15]

Courageous individuals also stepped forward to run blockades in pursuit of Bibles. Moses D. Hoge, who had been the pastor of the Second Presbyterian Church in Richmond since 1845, boarded a blockade-runner at Charleston in early 1863 bound for England. Hoge, as an emissary of the Virginia Bible Society, met Lord Shaftesbury, chairman of the British and Foreign Bible Society. The British counterpart to the American Bible Society gave Hoge a grant of ten thousand Bibles, fifty thousand New Testaments, and 250,000 portions of the Psalms and Gospels.[16]

Hoge had his Bibles in England, but now he and the Bibles had to return home. A Northern woman living in Richmond, a friend of the Hoge family, sent a message to the Union naval base at Hampton, Virginia. The Federals tracked his movements. Hoge decided to ship the Bibles in various quantities at different times. One ship with the Hoge Bibles was captured. His ship was fired upon, but he was able to arrive safely at Wilmington, North Carolina.[17]

The Bible became a precious cargo in time of war. Its importance simply meant that now *"both"* South and North would not only read but distribute their own Bibles.

———

How did Lincoln use and read the Bible? Are there any clues that might help us appreciate how he brings the Bible into play in such a prominent way in the Second Inaugural Address? There is agreement on the central place of the Bible in

Lincoln's early life in Kentucky and Indiana. The Bible may have been the only book the Lincoln family owned. While he was a young child, his parents joined the Separate Baptist church near their Knob Creek farm in Kentucky. The Separate Baptists were distinguished from the Regular Baptists in that they accepted no creed but the Bible. Mentor Graham, a schoolteacher who may have helped Lincoln study grammar in New Salem, told Herndon that the young Lincoln read "principally the Bible."[18]

Lincoln also learned as a child to commit favorite poems and passages of literature to memory. He memorized parts of Shakespeare's plays. It was his habit, as it was for many of his generation, to memorize not just individual verses but whole sections of Scripture. He seems to have been especially fond of the Psalms. Memorization was a part of the culture, but Lincoln became especially known for this practice.

In August and September 1841, Lincoln visited his best friend, Joshua F. Speed, at the Speed home near Louisville. Speed remembered Lincoln's mood upon his arrival as "very melancholy." Lucy Speed, Joshua's mother, observed Lincoln one day and was "pained at his deep depression." She decided to give Lincoln an Oxford edition of the King James Bible. In a letter to Herndon in 1866, Speed recalled how his mother had spoken to his friend about the Bible, "advising him to read it—to adopt its precepts and pray for its promises."[19]

The importance of this gift to a young Abraham Lincoln was confirmed twenty years later. President Lincoln received a request from Mrs. Lucy G. Speed in the fall of 1861 for a photograph. He replied:

For Mrs. Lucy G. Speed, from whose pious hand I accepted the present of an Oxford Bible twenty years ago.

A. Lincoln[20]

The testimony and reminiscences about Lincoln's use of the Bible in his adult years are conflicting. They must be sorted by evaluating the person who said them and when they were said. Immediately after Lincoln's death, his religious views became a battleground. Religion became a highly valued coin, as friends sought to claim a closeness of relationship to the growing stature of the martyred president.

Those who sought to Christianize Lincoln asserted that his frequent use of the Bible confirmed the orthodoxy of his Christian beliefs. On the other side were those who argued that, yes, Lincoln used the Bible, but principally as a literary source. From their standpoint, he drew from the Bible metaphors and quotations, but he did not use the Bible to articulate any particular theological point of view.

Many have reported that in his White House years Lincoln read the Bible frequently. Noah Brooks spent many hours in Lincoln's company at the White House. Within three months of Lincoln's death, he wrote in *Harper's Magazine,* "The Bible was a very familiar study with the President." Brooks reported that Lincoln "fixed in his memory" whole chapters from the New Testament, as well as from Isaiah and the Psalms. A favorite Lincoln practice was to "correct a misquotation of Scripture," quickly responding with "the chapter and verse where it could be found."[21]

Julia Taft Bayne, who turned sixteen on the day of Lincoln's first inauguration, became a friend of the Lincoln boys Tad and Willie. She and her younger brother and sister became favorite playmates at the White House. The Lincoln boys went with their parents to the New York Avenue Presbyterian Church, but soon they started going with Julia, Bud, and Holly Bayne to Fourth Presbyterian Church.

Frequently in the White House, Julia observed that Lincoln's big leather-covered Bible rested on a small table in the sitting room of the White House. She had a "distinct recollection" that "quite often," after the midday meal, Lincoln would sit sprawled out in his big chair in his large stocking feet reading the Bible. Mary Lincoln would sometimes protest against his habit of sitting in his stocking feet and order a servant to bring his slippers.[22]

Rebecca R. Pomoroy, a nurse who stayed in the White House with Mary Lincoln and Tad after Willie's death in 1862, confirms this general scene. Pomoroy recalled that Lincoln liked to recline on the couch while waiting for lunch and read from his mother's old worn-out Bible. One day Lincoln asked Pomoroy what book she liked to read best. "I am fond of the Psalms." "Yes," said Lincoln, "they are the best, for I find in them something for every day in the week."[23]

In the summer of 1864, Lincoln invited Joshua Speed to spend an evening with him at the Soldiers' Home. Starting in 1862, the Lincolns stayed in the tree-shaded Soldiers' Home, three miles north of the city boundary, from mid-June until October or even early November, while the weather was hot and humid. Lincoln rode the four miles from the White House to the Soldiers' Home each evening, either on horseback or in a small carriage with cavalry escort.

When Speed arrived, he found Lincoln sitting near a window in the stone cottage, one of the four buildings that constituted the Soldiers' Home, reading the Bible. Speed said, "I am glad to see you profitably engaged." "Yes," said Lincoln, "I am profitably engaged." "Well," Speed continued, "if you have recovered from your skepticism, I am sorry to say that I have not." With those words Lincoln rose, placed his hand on Speed's shoulder, and said, "You are wrong, Speed. Take all of this book upon reason that you can and the balance on faith, and you will live and die a happier and better man."[24] Speed described himself as a skeptic. In his reminiscences, he may well have wanted to magnify his relationship with Lincoln, but he would seem to have little incentive to build up Lincoln's use of the Bible.

Another incident involving Lincoln and the Bible occurred in September 1864. In the aftermath of the Emancipation Proclamation, there was a great outpouring of affection for Lincoln from African Americans. A black delegation from Baltimore had written in July to ask if they could come to the White House to present a Bible to the president. After their speech, Lincoln replied, "In regard to this Great Book, I have but to say, it is the best gift God has given to man. All the good the Saviour gave to the world was communicated through this book."[25]

Surely it is possible to read into Lincoln's remarks more than one motive. They may simply be gracious words by a wise politician to a group who made the Bible their best gift to the president. Or they may be heartfelt words from one who was discovering more of the wisdom of the Bible for himself as he sought to understand the whirlwind of war. However we assess Lincoln's words about the Bible, and the words of Lincoln's friends about Lincoln's use of the Bible, more important than any of these words is Lincoln's use of the Bible in his public speech.

After recognizing the use of the Bible and prayer by the soldiers on both sides, Lincoln, in a second level of meaning, went forward to probe the appropriate use of the Bible. Underneath this sentence was Lincoln's perception that the certainties in the Bible were now crashing into the uncertainties generated by the Civil War. Lincoln was entering into the crisis of how to read, interpret, and apply the Bible.

Lincoln, who had always had an ambivalent relationship with religion, suggested here that the Bible and prayer could be used almost as weapons to curry God's favor for one side or the other. He observed directly opposite readings of the Bible. On one side stood those who read a Bible that they steadfastly believed sanctioned slavery. On the other side were those who understood the Bible as encouraging the abolition of slavery.[26]

According to the letter to the Hebrews in the New Testament, "The word of God is quick, and powerful, and sharper than any two-edged sword." Lincoln liked to wield the Bible as a sword, using one edge to affirm and the other to question. Or, as the same verse continues, to use the other edge of the sword to judge "the thoughts and intents of the heart" (Hebrews 4:12, KJV).

In this second level of meaning, Lincoln judged "the thoughts and intents" of those who used or misused the Bible or prayer for partisan purposes. Lincoln offered here not only the edge of affirmation, but interrogation. The last part of the sentence, *"and each invokes His aid against the other,"* is not framed grammatically as a question, but it is clear that Lincoln now began a section where he asked questions about both human actions and God's actions.

Lincoln was asking how it was possible for one side to ask God's aid against the other side. He was not only asking a question, but inveighing against a tribal God who would take the side of a section or party. Lincoln was building a case for an inclusive God. He, who had been discontented with the sectarianism of the churches, was not happy with talk of a God who was captive to North or South. He had become troubled by those who came to him to say God was on our side. In his Second Inaugural, he spoke out against a tribal God, on the side of the North, and spoke instead of an inclusive God—inclusive, as Lincoln would explain, in both judgment and reconciliation.

As Lincoln had stood in a cold drizzle to say farewell to his friends in Springfield on February 11, 1861, he concluded his impromptu remarks by saying, "To His care commending you, as I hope in your prayers you will commend me, I bid you an affectionate farewell."[27] Lincoln, then in impromptu remarks, now in a prepared address, evoked the efficacy of prayer.

In public worship, Lincoln's practice was to stand while the pastoral prayer was being offered. Brooks, who arrived in Washington in the spring of 1861 as the reporter for the *Sacramento Bee,* first spied Lincoln as he stood to pray at the New York Avenue Presbyterian Church. It must have been quite a sight to see the tall president stand with bowed head for prayer.

Lincoln invoked prayer three times in the Second Inaugural.

> (1) *Both read the same Bible, and pray to the same God*
>
> (2) *The prayers of both could not be answered*
>   *that of neither has been answered fully*
>
> (3) *Fondly do we hope—fervently do we pray*

Lincoln commended both reading the Bible and praying by *"both sides."* However, even more directly than in his treatment of the Bible, the motive and practice of prayer were qualified and questioned.

> *The prayers of both could not be answered; that of neither has been answered fully.*

He was not saying not to pray. Brooks said that Lincoln told him "that after he went to the White House he kept up the habit of daily prayer. Sometimes it was only ten words, but those ten words he had."[28] Lincoln was saying here that the prayers of each side—to prevail against the other—*"could not be answered."* Lincoln the president now understood, as he may never have before the anguish of war, that *"neither has been answered fully."*

Lincoln was meaning that God must not be a tribal or territorial God. The pretension of human supplications in the practice of prayer now became the transition to what would become the major theological affirmation in Lincoln's entire address.

———

Integral to this Second Inaugural Address is an understanding of human nature. Building on years of experience and observation in his career as lawyer and politician, Lincoln offered an assessment of human behavior. He parried pretension and possibility.

The early focus was on pretension. Lincoln pointed out how *"strange that any men should dare to ask a just God's assistance in wringing their bread from the sweat of other men's faces."* He asked how it was possible for soldiers to read their Bibles and come up with such a *"strange"* practice as slavery, which went against all the precepts taught in the Bible.

Lincoln maintained a loving quarrel with the various Christian traditions that intersected his life. Whether it was Separate Baptist or Presbyterian, Lincoln was aware that religion, because of its appeal to the absolute, is capable of the most awful pretension by clothing immediate causes with ultimate sanction.

For Lincoln, the sanction of slavery from the Bible was the ultimate pretension. Newton Bateman, state superintendent of education in Illinois, told of a conversation with Lincoln in October 1860. They were examining a book containing a list of

Springfield voters. Lincoln told Bateman that he believed twenty of the twenty-three ministers in Springfield would vote against him in the upcoming presidential election. According to Bateman, Lincoln drew out a pocket New Testament and said, "It seems as if God had borne with this thing [slavery] until the very teachers of religion have come to defend it from the Bible, and to claim for it a divine character and sanction."[29]

Lincoln was aware of the use and abuse of the Bible by church leaders. The Protestant churches affirmed the Bible as their ultimate authority. That witness to the authority of the Bible took on a confrontational edge with the increasing numbers of Catholic immigrants arriving in the United States beginning in the 1830s. Protestants asserted the authority of the Bible, in contrast to the authority of the Catholic Pope. Catholics responded by chiding Protestants about the Bible as their paper Pope. Lincoln pointed out that, if the Bible was lauded as the formal authority for Protestant churches, in reality the clergy often functioned as the unacknowledged informal authority.

———

Lincoln pressed this point by invoking the first of four Biblical passages. He employed words from Genesis in which God orders Adam and Eve out of the Garden of Eden. Because they had disobeyed God, the lot of their daily life would be that

> In the sweat of thy face shalt thou eat bread
> [Genesis 3:19, KJV]

Here God was judging human beings. Lincoln used these words, surely familiar to his hearers, to start his case for the judgment of slavery. He had used this figure before. In debating Douglas in 1858, he connected it to a perennial struggle. "It is the eternal struggle between these two principles—right

and wrong—throughout the world. They are the two principles that have stood face to face from the beginning of
time. . . . One is the common right of humanity and the other
the divine right of kings." In challenging Douglas, Lincoln
used the Genesis figure: "It is the same spirit that says, 'You
work and toil and earn bread, and I eat it.'"[30]

Lincoln had experienced this kind of religion in an interview
three months before the Second Inaugural. In early December
1864, two women from Tennessee called upon the president to
ask for the release of their husbands, who were being held as
Confederate prisoners of war. Lincoln heard their story and
asked them to come back the next day. When they did so, one
of the women pleaded with Lincoln that "her husband was a
religious man." Lincoln objected: "In my opinion, the religion
that sets men to rebel and fight against their government, because, as they think, that government does not sufficiently help
some men to eat their bread on the sweat of *other* men's faces,
is not the sort of religion upon which people can get to
heaven!"[31] Lincoln asked the women to come back yet a third
day. With the conversations concluded, Lincoln had sat down
to write a summary of the interview for himself, perhaps wanting to retrieve this incident for later use. Hearing that Brooks
was in the parlor, Lincoln sent for him. Brooks came into the
library and found the president writing with a pencil on a piece
of common stiff boxboard. "Here is one speech of mine which
has never been printed, and I think it worth printing," Lincoln
told him. He gave his account of his interview to Brooks. With
a chuckle he added a caption, "The President's Last, Shortest,
and Best Speech." Brooks saw to it that this speech was printed
in the *Washington Daily Chronicle* on December 7, 1864.[32]
Less than three months later, this interview was surely in Lincoln's memory as he prepared his Second Inaugural. Certainly
he worked with the same text from Genesis as he pursued pretentiousness.

———

Through the years Lincoln had become critical of those who appealed to God on the basis of their own behavior. For the duration of this central paragraph, Lincoln would continue to work with the meanings of the justice and the judgment of God.

The theologian Reinhold Niebuhr wrote an article for *The Christian Century* that explored Lincoln's religious and political sensibilities. Niebuhr had come to believe that "Lincoln's religious convictions were superior in depth and purity to those held by the religious as well as by the political leaders of his day."[33] Niebuhr was well aware that this judgment could easily make him appear as just one more writer caught up in the kind of hagiography that ended up "substituting myths for sober reality" about our nation's heroes.

Niebuhr understood Lincoln's human achievement precisely because Lincoln's words included ambiguity. "Lincoln had a sense of historical meaning so high as to cast doubt on the intentions of both sides." Niebuhr believed this "human achievement" of Lincoln was unique among statesmen. Lincoln was able "to put the enemy into the same category of ambiguity as the nation to which his life was committed."[34]

Niebuhr appreciated Lincoln's ability in the Second Inaugural to balance moral judgments with religious reservations about the "partiality" of these judgments. Thus, Lincoln balanced the moral judgment:

> *It may seem strange that any men should dare to ask a just God's assistance in wringing their bread from the sweat of other men's faces;*

with the religious reservation:

but let us judge not that we be not judged. The prayers of
both could not be answered; that of neither have been an-
swered fully.

Niebuhr admired Lincoln's ability to embody political and
religious commitments and at the same time recognize the
"partiality of all historic commitments."[35]

———

As Lincoln buttressed his moral aversion to the South's embrace of slavery by quoting from the Old Testament, he balanced judgment with mercy by quoting from the New
Testament.

> Judge not, that ye be not judged.
> [Matthew 7:1, KJV]

These words come from Jesus' Sermon on the Mount, in
which he advocates an ethic rooted in humility and compassion. "Blessed are those" who do not follow the way of the
world, in this case judgment, but the new way of grace and
mercy.

The searing light of Lincoln's moral judgment is refracted
through a justice that is evenhanded. Lincoln, whose religion
has often been depicted as Old Testament in character, here
uses a teaching from the New Testament Sermon on the
Mount that offers explicit contrast to a legal understanding
of human relationships. This verse enjoins the hearer to practice mercy and humility.

It is this section that may have early on fastened the appel-
lation "Sermon on the Mount" to Lincoln's Second Inaugural
Address. Although only one of Lincoln's four quotations from

the Bible is from the Sermon on the Mount, the spirit of these teachings marks all his words.

As was common in Lincoln's use of Scripture, he made two subtle but significant changes. First, he added *"let us"* at the beginning of the injunction, making it at the same time less personal and more inclusive. Second, the substitution of *"we"* (*"be not judged"*) for the "ye" of the King James Version was also inclusive.

This second Biblical quotation is central. How we would like to hear Lincoln's tone as he quoted these words of Jesus. A speaker could employ such words just as a fencer might make a return thrust following a parry. If they are understood as a retaliatory sally, the intent of Lincoln's words is undermined. These words retain their integrity when used, as Lincoln did here, in humility and confession. Lincoln had earned the right to say these words by his own conduct over the course of four years of war.

The trajectory of this remark was thus toward the North. Northern politicians, press, and people had been harsh in their judgment of the South. Lincoln's struggle with the abolitionists was with the moral pretentiousness of their rhetoric. His dispute with the radical Republicans of his own party was over their intention to punish the South. His struggle with the churches was with their self-righteousness.

After Lincoln's death, a terrible spirit of judgment and retribution would be let loose on the South. Northern leaders would not heed his words. Lincoln's words asking that the nation *"judge not"* may have been appreciated in the short term, and would be remembered in the long term, but they were not acted upon.

6

"The Almighty has His own purposes."

The third paragraph continues:

The Almighty has His own purposes. "Woe unto the world because of offences! for it must needs be that offences come; but woe to that man by whom the offence cometh!" If we shall suppose that American Slavery is one of those offences{,} which, in the providence of God, must needs come, but which, having continued through His appointed time, He now wills to remove, and that He gives to both North and South, this terrible war, as the woe due to those by whom the offence came, shall we discern therein any departure from those divine attributes which the believers in a Living God always ascribe to Him?

On sultry days at the end of August 1862, Union and Confederate forces clashed in a fierce battle around Manassas Junction, a small railroad settlement on one of the main roads between Washington and Richmond. At Manassas, the Orange and Alexandria Railroad formed a junction with the Manassas Gap line proceeding west through the Blue Ridge to Strasburg. Thirteen months earlier, near the beginning of the war, the Union Army had suffered a disastrous defeat at this same place. In the North the battle was called Bull Run, the name of a meandering river several miles north.

Now, in the summer of 1862, John Pope, a West Pointer who was born in Kentucky and raised in Illinois, had been brought from the West and put in charge of the newly named Union Army of Virginia. In the last week of August, Stonewall Jackson, ever a gambler, marched his twenty-four thousand men fifty miles in two days to attack and burn the Union stacks of supplies at Manassas. Then Jackson's troops disappeared. Pope reported that he had Jackson on the run.

On the morning of August 29, Pope carried out disjointed attacks against Jackson. Next day, Lee and Jackson together fell upon Pope in what the North called the Second Battle of Bull Run. The Union troops broke and gave ground all the way to defenses on the outskirts of Washington. In five days of fighting, the Union forces of sixty-five thousand men suffered sixteen thousand casualties. Lee and Jackson's fifty-five thousand troops lost fewer than ten thousand men.[1] This defeat was a crushing blow. The South was jubilant. The Northern press reported deep discouragement and dissension.

Amid the public hand-wringing, the most public man in America met with his Cabinet officers. Attorney General Edward Bates captured Lincoln's somber mood in his diary entry for September 2. Bates wrote that the president was deeply discouraged after initial reports of victory had turned into news of a crushing defeat. Lincoln "seemed wrung by the bitterest anguish—said he felt almost ready to hang himself."[2]

That same day, Lincoln put pen to paper in a private musing. A brooding president strained to see the light in one of the darkest moments of the war:

> The will of God prevails. In great contests each party claims to act in accordance with the will of God. Both *may* be, and one *must* be wrong. God can not [sic] be *for*, and *against* the same thing at the same time. In the present civil war it is quite possible that God's purpose is something different from the purpose of either party—and yet the human instrumentalities, working just as they do, are of the best adaptation to effect His purpose.

I am almost ready to say this is probably true—that God wills this contest, and wills that it shall not end yet. By his mere quiet power, on the minds of the now contestants, He could have either *saved* or *destroyed* the Union without a human contest. Yet the contest began. And having begun He could give the final victory to either side any day. Yet the contest proceeds.[3]

This reflection remained unknown during Lincoln's life. Young John Hay, one of Lincoln's private secretaries, found it after his death. It was one of the few Lincoln papers that Hay kept for himself. In 1872, Hay gave it the title "Meditation on the Divine Will." The meditation revealed that Lincoln, at one of the most difficult moments in the war, was grappling to understand the meaning of the conflict in a new manner. This private meditation eloquently anticipated the affirmations of God's purposes at the core of the Second Inaugural Address.[4] (See appendix III.)

"The Almighty has His own purposes." With these words Lincoln brought the idea of God to the rhetorical center of his Second Inaugural Address. After discussing different actors, Lincoln concentrated on God as the primary actor. In quick strokes Lincoln described God's actions:

> *He now wills to remove*
>   *He gives to both North and South, this terrible war*
>   *Yet, if God wills that it continue*

This affirmation about God points both backward and forward: backward because it places in new light statements made early in the address about the purposes of different parties, forward to certain *"divine attributes"* of a *"Living God."*

In Lincoln's much-loved Shakespeare, as with any great

writer, one needs to progress to act III in order to understand the events and dialogue in act I. Just so, Lincoln was preparing his audience for his dramatic introduction of the *"purposes"* of a *"Living God"* by an earlier litany of human purposes in paragraphs one and two. We are now able to see that in Lincoln's first two paragraphs much more was taking place than historical description. Lincoln wanted his audience to understand the limitations of human purposes.

If we now bring all these *"purposes"* together, we can better appreciate Lincoln's strategy. His long litany included:

> *insurgent agents*
> > *one of them would <u>make</u> war*
> > > *the other would <u>accept</u> war*

We have heard that:

> *insurgents would rend the Union*
> > *the government claimed no right to do more*

and, finally,

> *Neither party expected for the war, the magnitude, or the duration*
> > *Neither anticipated that the <u>cause</u> of the conflict might cease*
> > > *Each looked for an easier triumph*
> > > > *Both read the same Bible, and pray to the same God*
> > > > *and each invokes His aid against the other*

With deft strokes Lincoln painted the motivations and actions of different parties. He did not exclude himself from this list. He was one of those who had *"looked for an easier triumph."* Each side believed its cause to be just, neither seemed willing to admit the partiality of its vision. The litany is meant to prepare us for a larger purpose.

From the moment Lincoln invoked the presence of God, questions abound. How could a person who had never joined a church use such language about God? Why did this language about God appear in the Second Inaugural when it was not present in the First Inaugural? What was the purpose?

Some have alleged that Lincoln adapted his words to the language of his audience. As an able and shrewd politician, Lincoln understood the marketplace. Religious language in the 1860s, coming on the heels of the Second Great Awakening, and still in the heat of abolitionism, was a major coin of the realm. Public expressions of piety, by preachers as well as political leaders, had become more prominent as the war went on. Lincoln knew he was speaking to a largely Protestant audience, and he adopted their language, so the argument goes. Therefore, Lincoln's admitted ability to read an audience accounted for both his invocation of God and his multiple use of Biblical texts.

Others have argued that religious values and language were simply a part of his Whig heritage. The Whig Party had always prided itself as "the party of moral probity, as an organization of church-going, sober, and respectable citizens." They stigmatized the Democrats as "godless and immoral." Some had even called the Whig Party the "Christian party." The new Republican Party wanted to capitalize on its reputation as the party of Protestant moral values. If the Republican Party was not in any simple sense "the Christian party in politics," Richard J. Carwardine has argued that "for northern antislavery evangelicals it deserved the mantle far more than any party in the republic's history."[5]

Still others claim that Lincoln excluded beliefs or language that would have put off his audience. Thus, his address did not draw upon Enlightenment ideas about God, often expressed in the language of fatalism. Donald, in *Lincoln,* argues that the author of the Second Inaugural wanted to use other words. "He might have put his argument in terms of the doctrine of necessity, in which he had long believed, but that was not a dogma accepted by most Americans." Donald observes, "Addressing a devout, Bible-reading public, Lincoln knew he would be understood when he invoked the familiar doctrine of exact retribution, the belief that the punishment for a violation of God's law would equal the offense itself."[6]

None of these proposals offers an adequate explanation for Lincoln's ideas and language, or takes into account the evolution of Lincoln's thinking and ideas during the turbulent years of the Civil War. To get at the meaning of Lincoln's words, we need to examine the origins of Lincoln's theological language. We can know more about the origins of his ideas than the audience knew that day. He was his own editor, adapting and revising materials he had used before. In this examination of sentences in paragraph three, we will encounter ideas and language that go back to the "Meditation on the Divine Will" and other earlier letters and interviews. These literary antecedents are evidence of Lincoln's ongoing wrestling with the purposes of God.

———

The "Meditation on the Divine Will" occupies a central place in our attempt to understand the mind of Lincoln in the years that led up to the Second Inaugural Address.

First, this private reflection is evidence of a fundamental shift in Lincoln's approach to the war before it was revealed in public. The "Meditation" discloses that sixteen months into the Civil War Lincoln was already beginning to think in fresh ways.

Second, because the "Meditation" was private, with no intention that it would ever become public, it becomes a primary resource in answering the question of the integrity of Lincoln's ideas in the Second Inaugural. We see that Lincoln's ideas about God's will and purpose were not developed simply to appeal to an audience in March 1865.

Lincoln began his private musing with a simple declaration: "The will of God prevails." One strains to understand the feeling and emotion with which Lincoln started this reflection. Did he write in a spirit of resignation? Were these, rather, words of affirmation? Or both?

In comparing the "Meditation on the Divine Will" with the Second Inaugural, we see both continuity and development.

"MEDITATION ON THE DIVINE WILL"	SECOND INAUGURAL ADDRESS
The will of God prevails.	*The Almighty has His own purposes.*
Both *may* be, and one *must* be wrong. God can not [sic] be *for,* and *against* the same thing at the same time.	*The prayers of both could not be answered; that of neither has been answered fully.*
I am almost ready to say this is probably true—that God wills this contest, and wills that it shall not end.	*He now wills to remove* *Yet, if God wills that it continue*

If we compare the texts, the continuity is more in ideas than in exact language. In both texts Lincoln was thinking about a God who wills. In the "Meditation," he writes four times about either "the will of God" or "God wills." In the Second Inaugural, he speaks about *"God wills"* twice, both in connection with the *"offence"* of slavery.

If the "Meditation" was philosophical or speculative in spirit, by the Second Inaugural Lincoln sounded more settled in his convictions. He was more concrete. After pondering in the "Meditation" how it was that both sides claimed "to act in accordance with the will of God," Lincoln answered his own question by stating, "Both *may* be, and one *must* be wrong." By 1865, Lincoln made this general philosophical problem more concrete by invoking the image of soldiers praying, *"The prayers of both could not be answered."*

———

When the Lincolns came to Washington in late February 1861, they were courted by a number of churches. On March 6, 1861, two days after the First Inaugural Address, the First Presbyterian Church invited President and Mrs. Lincoln to accept a pew in their church. Rent-free. First Presbyterian was a church made up largely of Democrats and included many of the Southern members of Congress. Lincoln declined to join.[7]

Montgomery Blair, the new postmaster general, may have been the one who pointed the Lincolns toward the New York Avenue Presbyterian Church. In 1859, the F Street Presbyterian and Second Presbyterian Churches had merged to become the New York Avenue Presbyterian Church. A deacon from the New York Avenue church brought a plat or map of the pews over to the White House for inspection. No free rent. The annual rental of the pew would be fifty dollars a year. The Lincoln family attended New York Avenue Presbyterian on March 10, the first Sunday after the inauguration.[8]

The fact that Lincoln never formally joined a church has been used to question his words about God, the Bible, and faith. What needs to be remembered is that Lincoln, in both Springfield and Washington, was drawn to Presbyterian churches. He participated in Old School Presbyterian churches.

1

This photograph of Abraham Lincoln was taken by Alexander Gardner in Washington on Sunday, February 5, 1865, one month before the Second Inaugural Address. For many years the photograph was misdated as five days before Lincoln's death and thus the last picture of him. This same photograph appears on the simple Lincoln ribbon from the Second Inaugural celebrations.

2

This photograph and the drawing below depict two quite different views of the Second Inaugural. Here the crowd is standing in the rain and mud. The wooden platform, extending from the east front of the Capitol, is barely visible in the upper left.

3

This idealized drawing of the inaugural ceremonies, as shown in *Frank Leslie's Illustrated Newspaper* (March 18, 1865), is dominated by the recently completed dome of the Capitol with Armed Liberty on top. Contrast the dress of the spectators in the photograph and the drawing.

Frederick Douglass, abolitionist reformer and editor, was extremely critical of Lincoln's First Inaugural Address. He then had the opportunity to speak with Lincoln at the White House in 1863 and 1864, and came to the Second Inaugural eager to hear what the president would say.

Walt Whitman, beginning to become known for the first editions of *Leaves of Grass,* observed Lincoln on numerous occasions. Whitman became convinced that no artist or photographer could capture the deep meaning in Lincoln's face.

Walt Whitman
Washington DC
1863

Phineas Densmore Gurley was the minister of the New York Avenue Presbyterian Church in Washington where Abraham and Mary Lincoln worshipped. Gurley is a forgotten figure in our attempt to understand the sources of Lincoln's ideas.

6

Eliza P. Gurney, Quaker reformer from Philadelphia, visited Lincoln in the White House in October 1862. She and Lincoln then carried on a correspondence, in which he articulated ideas about the purposes of God in language similar to that of the Second Inaugural.

7

8

The United States Christian Commission, formed in 1862, became the main distributor of American Bible Society Bibles during the war. In this drawing, a Christian Commission worker, in the course of distributing Bibles, reads to a soldier in the field.

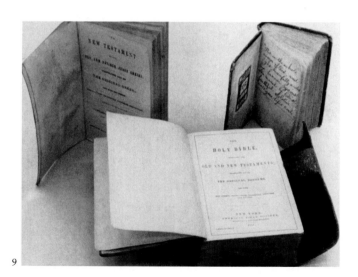

9

In the Second Inaugural Lincoln stated, "Both read the same Bible." This display shows three Bibles used by soldiers in the Civil War. The American Bible Society's complete *Holy Bible* (IN FOREGROUND) was printed in 1861. The Bible Society of the Confederate States of America printed the *New Testament* (LEFT) in 1863.

The ABS *New Testament* (RIGHT) carries the inscription, "Put on the whole armor of God, and fight manfully under his banner against Sin and be Christ's faithful Soldier unto your lifes [sic] end."

11

A simple ribbon made in the United States includes the Alexander Gardner photograph of Lincoln of February 5, 1865. Both of these ribbons would have been sold or distributed on and surrounding March 4, 1865.

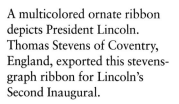

10

A multicolored ornate ribbon depicts President Lincoln. Thomas Stevens of Coventry, England, exported this stevens-graph ribbon for Lincoln's Second Inaugural.

IN THIS TEMPLE
AS IN THE HEARTS OF THE PEOPLE
FOR WHOM HE SAVED THE UNION
THE MEMORY OF ABRAHAM LINCOLN
IS ENSHRINED FOREVER

The complete text of the Second Inaugural is inscribed on the north wall at the Lincoln Memorial in Washington, D.C. Since the memorial opened in 1922, Daniel Chester French's magnificent statue of Lincoln has greeted visitors from around the world. The statue of Lincoln has served as the backdrop for important national events, including Martin Luther King Jr.'s "I Have a Dream" speech in August 1963.

13

The only photograph we have of Lincoln speaking was taken at the Second Inaugural. In the assemblage, captured by Alexander Gardner on March 4, 1865, is everyone from cabinet officers and congressmen to Union soldiers and Confederate deserters. John Wilkes Booth can be seen to the right of center and above, hatless, facing the camera.

The Presbyterian church in the United States had divided in 1837 into Old and New School denominations, the split occurring over a number of theological and organizational issues. Both traditions sought to be grounded in the Bible, but the Old School remained rooted in a doctrinal tradition, whereas the New School was open to experience expressed in the enthusiasms of revivalism. Differing beliefs about slavery and the church's political and social roles were an issue. The New School was more attuned to antislavery politics. A strong element within the Old School held a point of view that the church, as a spiritual institution, should not involve itself in political questions.[9]

From his earliest years, Lincoln had been wary of emotion, as evidenced in his warnings in his Address Before the Young Men's Lyceum of Springfield in 1838. As a young adult, he had embraced the use of reason, honed through his training as a lawyer. I believe he sought and found two Presbyterian preachers who were thoughtful and reasonable in their approach to faith. Both pastors embodied the constellation of ideas and practices that came to be identified with Old School Presbyterianism.

———

In Springfield, the Lincolns were drawn first to the Reverend James Smith and later to his congregation, the First Presbyterian Church. At the time of the death of their son, Edward B. Lincoln, Mary was worshipping occasionally at St. Paul's Episcopal Church. The Reverend Charles Dresser, the Episcopal minister, had performed their marriage in 1842. At the time of Eddie's death, Dresser was away from Springfield and it was Smith who offered pastoral comfort to Abraham and Mary Lincoln. The Presbyterian minister conducted Eddie's funeral on February 1, 1850. Two years later, in 1852, Mary joined the First Presbyterian Church. The Lincolns rented pew number 20 in the fifth row of the church. Thomas (Tad) Lincoln was baptized at First Presbyterian in 1856.

Lincoln attended the First Presbyterian Church in Springfield infrequently. Sometimes he was away, traveling on the Eighth Circuit while building his career as a lawyer. It is a matter of disputed memory exactly how often he did attend when he was in town. Lincoln did accept an appointment by the session of First Presbyterian in 1853 as one of three lawyers asked to assist Dr. Smith in a suit in the local presbytery. Since it was contrary to the Presbyterian discipline to allow outside counsel in such suits, it would have been understood that Lincoln was related to First Presbyterian Church.[10]

James Smith had developed a reputation for learned preaching. As a young man, like Lincoln, Smith had been intrigued with the ideas of such thinkers as Constantin Volney and Thomas Paine. Smith had migrated in his faith pilgrimage through the Cumberland Presbyterian Church, a group whose emphasis on revivalism and experience had affinities to New School Presbyterians. He came to rest in Old School Presbyterianism in the 1840s.

The theme of Smith's ministry was his commitment to a reasonable faith. In 1843, he wrote *The Christian's Defence, Containing a Fair Statement, and Impartial Examination of the Leading Objections Urged by Infidels Against the Antiquity, Genuineness, Credibility, and Inspiration of the Holy Scriptures.* The book grew out of debates in 1841 with a popular "freethinker," Charles G. Olmstead. Smith and Olmstead debated for eighteen successive evenings at Columbus, Mississippi.[11]

Not long after Eddie's death, the Lincolns traveled to Kentucky to stay with Mary's relatives. At the Todd home, Lincoln is believed to have read portions of Smith's 650-page treatise. In *The Christian's Defence,* Smith aimed to defend above all the authority and truthfulness of the Old and New Testaments. In critiquing contemporary deviations from true faith, he was concerned that "the exercises of the under-standing must be separated from the tendencies of the fancy, or of the heart." Surely this was a reference to the emotional, revivalistic faith from which he had only recently emerged. Ninian W. Edwards, who was married to Mary Todd Lincoln's older sister, Elizabeth, reported that Lincoln told him that as a result of reading Smith's book he was now "convinced of the truth of the Christian religion."[12]

Smith's approach must have appealed to Lincoln's penchant for logic and reasonableness. Lincoln, put off by the emotionalism he witnessed in the revivalistic religion of his youth, would have agreed with Smith's recommendation that in the approach to religion "the mind must be trained to the hardihood of abstract and unfeeling intelligence." Smith argued that in matters of faith "everything must be given up to the supremacy of argument."[13]

Lincoln's participation at the New York Avenue Presbyterian Church coincided with his deepening struggles to understand the meaning of God's activity in the maelstrom of war. Precisely at the moment that internal evidence points to the ferment in Lincoln's thinking, he was listening to one of the best models of Old School Presbyterian theology in preaching. Phineas Densmore Gurley, a handsome man of large frame and voice, had graduated from Princeton Theological Seminary in 1840. He served churches in Indianapolis and Dayton, Ohio, before being called to Washington in 1854.

In May 1860, the very month when the Republicans were gathering in Chicago to nominate Lincoln as their candidate for president, Gurley received a letter from Princeton Seminary. Twenty years after his graduation, Princeton was seeking someone to be responsible for "the preaching and pastoral department." Professor Alexander T. McGill wrote Gurley of the pressing need "to tender the Pastoral department to some good pastor. What would you think of it?" Professor McGill proposed nominating Gurley.[14] The invitation from Princeton Seminary indicated the esteem for Gurley, who was building a reputation as a preacher and pastor.

We have no record of Gurley's response, but Gurley soon found himself with another calling. From the spring of 1861 to the spring of 1865, he preached to Abraham Lincoln, officiated at Willie Lincoln's funeral, prayed beside the dying president, and preached the funeral sermon for the martyred president at the Executive Mansion. Whereas some have pointed to the influence of pastor James Smith at First Presbyterian Church of Springfield, President Lincoln had more frequent interchange with Phineas Densmore Gurley. He is an overlooked figure in the Lincoln story.

———

Gurley stood squarely in the American Old School Presbyterian understanding of Reformed theology. Three classical traditions—Lutheran, Reformed, and Anglican—grew from the Reformation of the sixteenth century. Their similarities were much greater than their differences, but each tradition recovered and emphasized certain aspects of the church universal.

The basic themes of Reformed or Calvinist theology were shaped by John Calvin in Geneva and handed down through Calvinists in England, Scotland, and Holland. God was understood not as the first principle in philosophy, but as the primary actor in history. Persecuted in old Europe and old England, in the New World, Calvinists, as Pilgrims, Puritans, and Presbyterians, sought to live under the kingly rule of God; balancing their high view of God was a low view of humanity. The paradox was that their belief in the sinfulness of human beings did not lead to passivity, because they were confident that in God's sovereign rule human beings were instruments of divine purpose.

At the hub of the Reformed theological tradition in the United States was Princeton Theological Seminary, founded in 1812. In its first decades, the Princeton faculty worried both about the aridity of deism and the enthusiasm of revivalism. Princeton's founding faculty's answer was an educated clergy trained in Reformed theology.

Gurley came to study at Princeton just as Charles Hodge was starting to build his reputation as a leading Reformed theologian. Hodge has often been remembered for a comment he offered in 1872, at the celebration honoring his fifty years of teaching on the faculty at Princeton. "I am not afraid to say that a new idea never originated in this seminary."[15] This remark has always been good for a laugh. Hodge's intention had been to maintain the Reformed tradition. Central to this American Reformed tradition was providence. In defense of providence, Hodge and his students were prepared to combat deviations from historic Christianity.

———

Modern biographers have focused on fatalism to understand Lincoln's religious thought. Fatalism is the belief that all events take place in accordance with unvarying laws of causation. The popular expression of fatalism is that whatever happens is bound to happen. The form of fatalism that Lincoln encountered in the early nineteenth century asked him to resign himself to a course of events outside his control. Fatalism fit well with the advent of deism in the eighteenth century, which denied the involvement of God in the affairs of history.

Biographer Stephen Oates (1977) describes the young Lincoln in 1833 as "a religious fatalist like his mother." Donald

(1995) invokes Lincoln's fatalism to support his thesis of "Lincoln's reluctance to take the initiative and make bold plans." Donald argues that Lincoln, from his earliest days, "had a sense that his destiny was controlled by some larger force, some Higher Power."[16]

Oates conjectures that this belief in fatalism continued into the Lincoln presidency. Many have pointed to the death of Willie on February 20, 1862, as a critical moment in Lincoln's struggles with faith. "After Willie's death, he talked more frequently about God than he had before," Oates wrote, but he averred that the only change was that "his fatalism was more intense and more deeply felt."[17]

Fatalism was often associated with the doctrine of necessity. Lincoln ran as a Whig for Congress in the summer of 1846. In the midst of this campaign, he was accused of being "a scoffer at Christianity" by his Methodist-minister opponent, Peter Cartwright. Lincoln produced a handbill directed to the voters of the Seventh Congressional District in which he attempted to answer the charge. He stated that in his earlier years he "was inclined to believe in what I understand is called the 'Doctrine of Necessity.'" He then offered this definition: "The human mind is impelled to action, or held in rest by some power, over which the mind has no control."[18]

Herndon liked to point to Lincoln's early experiences in the Baptist church as a source of his law partner's fatalism. Lincoln's parents had joined the Little Mount Separate Baptist Church in Kentucky. The Separate Baptists, known also as the Primitive Baptists, believed in a radical predestinarian theology. God was the only real actor. There was absolutely no free will. The Separate Baptists had no mission boards for evangelism. They believed that God had already determined from the foundation of the world who would be converted.[19]

This earliest Baptist experience should not bear too much weight. Allen Guelzo, in his biography, *Abraham Lincoln:*

Redeemer President, demonstrates that Lincoln, as a man of ideas, had access to multiple intellectual sources in the 1830s and 1840s that formed his beliefs. The younger Lincoln's reading included Thomas Paine's *Age of Reason,* Constantin-François Volney's *Ruins, or a Survey of the Revolution of Empires,* and Robert Chambers's *Vestiges of the Natural History of Creation.* Lincoln's interest in political economy led him to read the English liberal John Stuart Mill's *Principles of Political Economy.*

In 1846, Lincoln discovered in a newspaper the poem "Mortality" and was instantly drawn to it. He did not at the time know that the poem was by William Knox, a Scot. He memorized its fifty-six lines and recited it frequently.

President Zachary Taylor died of cholera in July 1850. Lincoln traveled to Chicago and offered a eulogy for the old general. He concluded by quoting six stanzas from "Mortality."

So the multitude goes, like the flower or the weed,
That withers away to let others succeed;
So the multitude comes, even those we behold,
To repeat every tale that has often been told.

For we are the same, our fathers have been,
We see the same sights our fathers have seen;
We drink the same streams and see the same sun
And run the same course our fathers have run.

They loved; but the story *we* cannot unfold;
They scorned, but the heart of the haughty is cold;
They grieved, but no wail from their slumbers will come,
They joyed, but the tongue of their gladness is dumb.

They died! Aye, they died; we things that are now;
That work on the turf that lies on their brow,

And make in their dwellings a transient abode,
Meet the things that they met on their pilgrimage road.

Yea! Hope and despondency, pleasure and pain,
Are mingled together in sun-shine and rain;
And the smile and the tear, and the song and the dirge,
Still follow each other, like surge upon surge.

'Tis the wink of an eye, 'tis the draught of a breath,
From the blossoms of health, to the paleness of death.
From the gilded saloon, to the bier and the shroud.
Oh, why should the spirit of mortal be proud![20]

This poetry, with its invocation of eternal and unchanging rhythms of life, must have spoken to Lincoln as a man who had incurred tremendous losses in his life. He lost his mother in 1818, when he was nine years old. His sister Sally died in childbirth in 1828, when she was twenty-one. At twenty-six, he was plunged into depression when Ann Rutledge, a young woman from New Salem whom he apparently loved deeply, died suddenly.

After he married Mary Todd in 1842, death continued to strike those whom Lincoln loved the most. His son Edward died of what was probably pulmonary tuberculosis in 1850. His son Willie died of bronchial pneumonia in 1862 at the White House. In Lincoln's recurrent bouts with melancholy, some allege that fatalism touched his sense of sadness. Or did his sadness trigger fatalism?

Historians and biographers have too often equated fatalism and providence. Nineteenth-century writers would not have made that judgment. The two constellations of ideas had different origins and different outcomes. Fatalism and providence might appear to be cousins, but the theologians and pastors of that era were sure to tell you that they were not the same.

In 1859 Francis Wharton wrote *A Treatise on Theism and the Modern Skeptical Theories* to make just this point. Wharton, who would become one of the first professors at the Episcopal Theological Seminary in Cambridge, Massachusetts, characterized fatalism as "a distinct scheme of unbelief" because it failed to recognize the personality and action of a loving God. By contrast, Wharton characterized the God of Christianity by "his watchful care and love."[21]

For Hodge, the recognition of the personality of God was the key to the distinction between providence and fatalism. In his treatment of God's "government," Hodge argued, "This doctrine necessarily flows from the Scriptural idea of God. He is declared to be a personal being, infinite in wisdom, goodness, and power." In his three-volume *Systematic Theology*, Hodge said of providence, "An infinitely wise, good, and powerful God is everywhere present, controlling all events great and small, necessary, and free, in a way perfectly consistent with the nature of his creatures and with his own infinite excellence." In fatalism, events unfold according to certain laws of nature. In Christian theology, God's divine power is able to embrace human freedom and responsibility.[22]

A clear statement about the relationship of providence and fatalism came on the occasion of remembering one of the South's leading heroes of the Civil War. "Stonewall" Jackson was renowned not only as Lee's right arm in the armies of the Confederacy, but as a Presbyterian deacon and Sunday-school teacher. On the night of May 2, 1863, Jackson, with a few of his officers, rode beyond Confederate lines to try to gain information about Union positions on the Plank Road near Chancellorsville, Virginia. As he and his party rode back toward their own lines, they were mistaken for federal cavalry and fired upon. Three bullets struck Jackson. At first there was hope that Jackson would recover, but he died on Sunday, May 10. His death severely tested the South's belief that God was on their side.[23]

Jackson became one of the first Southern heroes memorialized in stone after the war. Moses Drury Hoge, minister of the Second Presbyterian Church, spoke at the unveiling of the statue of Stonewall Jackson on Capitol Square in Richmond on October 26, 1875. Hoge, who had been a frequent correspondent with Charles Hodge, spoke at length about Jackson's abiding trust in God's providence. He called this belief in providence "surely the primary fact, the supreme fact in the history of General Jackson." He added, "I cannot leave the subject without adding that those who confound his faith in Providence with fatalism, mistake both the spiritual history of the man and the meaning of the very words they employ." Hoge was determined to make the point that for anyone nurtured within the Presbyterian tradition there could be no identification of providence with fatalism.[24]

———

Lincoln became more regular in his church attendance in Washington. Early on, his children went with their playmates Julia, Bud, and Holly Bayne to Fourth Presbyterian Church, but Lincoln did not accompany them to this New School Presbyterian congregation. One of his requirements for choosing a minister and a church had to do with politics, or the lack of it. In consulting Montgomery Blair, Lincoln is reported to have said, "I wish to find a church whose clergyman holds himself aloof from politics." Perhaps he had had enough of those clergymen in Springfield who were too often Democrats preaching against him and his politics. When asked about Gurley and his sermons, Lincoln is said to have retorted, "I like Gurley. He don't preach politics. I get enough of that through the week, and when I go to church, I like to hear the gospel."[25]

Lincoln did hear Gurley preach sermons that accented the theme of providence. The new president was present for worship at New York Avenue on April 14, 1861. He must surely have come to church that Sunday with foreboding. On Friday, April 12, Confederate troops had opened fire on Fort Sumter. After thirty-three hours of fighting, the American flag would be lowered on Sunday, April 14. Lincoln had wrestled with issuing a proclamation calling for seventy-five thousand troops in order to "redress wrongs long enough endured." The news from Charleston had spread both gloom and anger across the city. In the sermon, Lincoln heard Gurley appeal to God's providence. "God, in His merciful providence had afforded another opportunity for counsel, for pause, for appeal to Him for assistance before letting loose upon the land the direst scourge which He permits to visit a people—civil war."[26]

Within the first year of the Civil War, William Wallace Lincoln fell ill and died in February 1862. Of all Lincoln's sons, Willie was most like his father, in both looks and character. Lincoln was overcome with grief, and in his sorrow had several conversations with Dr. Gurley. On February 24, Gurley presided at a funeral service for Willie at the White House.

Gurley centered his sermon on what was finally "very comforting"—namely, "to get a clear and a scriptural view of the providence of God." The meaning of this divine providence was that "His kingdom ruleth over all." Gurley, in the spirit of Hodge, was not announcing some wooden, arbitrary providence. He acknowledged the perplexity of providence, calling it "a mysterious dealing." Yet, in his final words of comfort, Gurley invited the president to "bow in *His* presence with an humble and teachable spirit; only let us be still and know that He is God."[27] In such a moment, which anyone who has suffered the death of a child knows is an occa-

sion of grief beyond words, Gurley offered words with a remarkable affinity to those that Lincoln was beginning to use
himself.

Lincoln was present on August 6, 1863, at New York Avenue when Gurley preached a sermon in response to the president's call for a national day for public humiliation, prayer,
and fasting. Gurley's sermon, "Man's Projects and God's Results," began with a text: Proverbs 16:9. "A man's heart de-
viseth his way: but the Lord directs his steps." At the outset,
Gurley recognized the growing debate between human
agency and divine providence. He set up the debate in the
first two paragraphs. "Man is a rational, a free, and, therefore an accountable moral agent." And added, "But while
this is true, it is also true that God governs the world." He
went on to affirm, "He accomplishes His fixed and eternal
purpose through the instrumentality of free, and accountable, and even *wicked* agents."[28]

Gurley, in his sermons, called attention to the potential
logical contradiction of free agency and God's governance.
By the use of various metaphors, he heightened, not lessened,
this paradox. "Man devises; the Lord directs." Or "man
*pro*poses; God *dis*poses." Again, "man's agency, and God's
overruling sovereignty." Gurley chose this theme of human
agency and God's sovereignty, he said, as the best way to understand "the probable fruits and consequences of the terrible struggle" in which the nation had been engaged.[29]

These three sermons represent Gurley's theology and
preaching. All three were preached when we know Lincoln
was in attendance. A fellow minister described Gurley's ministry as "Calvinism presented in his beautiful examples and
spirit and preaching."[30] His sermons returned again and again
to the Calvinist emphasis on providence, albeit usually acknowledging the elements of ambiguity and mystery in dis-
cerning that providence.

In the final years of the Civil War, Lincoln began attending the midweek evening prayer service held in the main lecture room at New York Avenue. It was reported that he sat in the pastor's study with the door partially ajar, but within hearing distance. The themes that he heard are strikingly similar to some of the ideas about providence that he was just then developing in his own, more distinctive language and cadences.

———

Preaching on providence was certainly not the exclusive province of Presbyterians. Another window into Lincoln's changing thinking about providence opens onto an unusual relationship with a Quaker woman. In October 1862, Eliza P. Gurney, a Quaker minister from Philadelphia, convened a prayer meeting in the president's office. She and three friends had waited two days for an interview with the president for the purposes of comforting and exhorting him. At first the president thought Mrs. Gurney was from England.

Lincoln was sympathetic to the plight of the Quakers. As pacifists they hated war, but he knew they had been among the earliest antislavery advocates in the nation. After preaching a sermon about the need to seek divine guidance, Mrs. Gurney knelt and offered a prayer "that light and wisdom might be shed down from on high, to guide our President."[31]

Quakerism was badly divided. While still in her twenties, Gurney had spoken throughout the United States exhorting evangelical Quakers to stand firm against a more liberal group known as Hicksites. The lines were drawn over such issues as the authority of the Bible and the divinity of Christ. Later, on a tour of England, she met and married Joseph John Gurney, a Norwich banker and philanthropist, who was the leading Friend in England. The group supporting an evangelical Quakerism would come to be called Gurneyites.

Lincoln, who was usually closemouthed about his deepest feelings, was remarkably open in revealing his thoughts and feelings to Eliza Gurney. In commenting on their first meeting, he observed, "If I had my way, this war would never have commenced. If I had been allowed my way this war would have ended before this, but we find it still continues."[32] These remarks indicate that Lincoln, by the fall of 1862, was becoming more circumspect about his power to affect the course of the war.

One focus of Lincoln's conversation and correspondence with Gurney over the next several years was the dimensions of God's providence and purposes. Lincoln offered an affirmation to Gurney that was in the same tenor as the "Meditation." "We must believe that He permits it [the war] for some wise purpose of his own, mysterious and unknown to us; and though with our limited understandings we may not be able to comprehend it, yet we cannot but believe, that he who made the world still governs it." In October 1862, these purposes of God were "mysterious and unknown." Yet Lincoln was becoming more confident that there was a purpose. In a crisis of government, Lincoln employed the language of government to speak of God's rule, "he who made the world still governs it."[33]

On August 18, 1863, Gurney wrote to Lincoln from Earlham Lodge, her summer home, near Atlantic City, New Jersey. She had long been an antislavery advocate. In the afterglow of the Emancipation Proclamation, she wrote to assure Lincoln of "the prayer of many thousands" whose hearts had been "gladdened by thy praiseworthy and *successful* effort 'to burst the bands of wickedness, and let the oppressed go free.'"[34]

On September 4, 1864, after an unexplained lapse of more than a year, Lincoln resumed his correspondence with Mrs.

Gurney. The summer of 1864 had brought new anxieties in the North. On July 11, Confederate General Jubal Early led fifteen thousand Confederate troops to within five miles of the White House. Lincoln himself had been in jeopardy when a bullet whistled by as he stood on the parapet at Fort Stevens.

After a summer of bad news, good news arrived at the beginning of September with the capture of Atlanta by Sherman. Whatever the news, Lincoln seemed more self-assured about the purposes of God than he had been two years earlier, in his first letter to Gurney. He now wrote her, "The purposes of the Almighty are perfect," an affirmation that compares to the words in the Second Inaugural, *"The Almighty has His own purposes."*

Lincoln now seemed convinced that those purposes "must prevail, though we erring mortals may fail to accurately perceive them in advance." He expressed both his hopes and his resignation. "We hoped for a happy termination of this terrible war long before this; but God knows best, and has ruled otherwise."

In the period during which Lincoln wrote this letter, he was straining to understand, from the standpoint of divine purpose, what good could come from a terrible war. "Meanwhile we must work earnestly in the best light He gives us, trusting that so working still conduces to the great ends He ordains. Surely He intends some great good to follow this mighty convulsion, which no mortal could make, and no mortal could stay." Exactly six months to the day before March 4, 1865, Lincoln's second letter to Gurney foreshadowed the ideas and the language of the Second Inaugural.[35]

Though praising the inscrutable intentions of God in his Second Inaugural Address, Lincoln did not retreat to agnosticism about the specific content of those purposes. He focused those purposes in the Second Inaugural by invoking a fiery Biblical quotation. In his brooding he had discerned that the purposes of God could also bring judgment. Lincoln now borrowed a third passage from the Bible.

> Woe unto the world because of offences! for it must needs be that offences come; but woe to that man by whom the offence cometh!
>
> [Matthew 18:7, KJV]

When Lincoln spoke the word *"offences,"* he shifted the tone of his address. The feeling tone of *"offences"* jolts us. In defining *"American Slavery"* as one of *"those offences"* against God, Lincoln broadened out the historical and emotional range of his address.

The word "offence" in the Greek of the New Testament is *skandalon*. What the King James Version translated as "offence," today's New Revised Standard Version translates as "stumbling block." This verse in Matthew's Gospel is part of a series of teachings by Jesus about how to treat the "little ones"—members of the Christian community who were immature in faith. These persons were not to be treated with disdain, but were to be watched over with great consideration. One must lead one's life so as not to be a "stumbling block" to the weaker members of the community.

Whether or not Lincoln was aware of the larger context of this verse, he seems to have captured part of its essential spirit. He had long believed that slavery was evil at its core because one person held another in bondage. He arrived more slowly at the conclusion that slavery was evil in its circumference, for it propagated still other evils. Whereas for a long time he had been willing to contain slavery politically and geographically, he had come to the conclusion in the midst of the Civil War that its moral implications could not be contained. Slavery made a lie of democratic principles.

"If we shall suppose that American Slavery is one of those offences." What was there and then in the Bible had become here and now in *"American Slavery."* In using this second passage from the Gospel of Matthew, Lincoln employed the sanction of Scripture to initiate his indictment of slavery, and ultimately his formal charge against the American people.

Lincoln did not say "Southern Slavery." By saying *"American Slavery,"* Lincoln asserted that North and South must together own the offense. He was not simply trying to set the historical record straight. He was thinking of the future. Lincoln understood, as many in his own party did not, that the Southern people would never be able to take their full places in the Union if they felt that they alone were saddled with the guilt for what was the national offense of slavery.

One of the major foundations in the house of slavery was that it had always been and would always be. However strange it is to our ears today, proponents of slavery in Lincoln's day argued that the master-slave relationship was a natural relation that must be preserved. Lincoln took this point of view head-on by countering that slavery had *now* run its appointed course in history.

Lincoln offered a Biblical and theological sanction for declaring that slavery must *now* come to an end. Starting in 1854, he began to appeal to Jefferson's words in the Declaration of Independence, "All men are created equal," as a warrant for advocating political rights for blacks. Now, in 1865,

Lincoln appealed to Jesus' words in the Bible as a warrant that the time for slavery had *now* come and gone.

All through the war, a vexing question was whether a war begun to preserve the Union could be transformed into a war to end slavery. General McClellan excoriated Lincoln, literally shouting that the president and government had no right to change the announced intention of fighting the war to preserve the Union. Many in the military were initially angry that a fight to free the slaves was not why they had volunteered at the beginning of the war. The copperheads or peace Democrats expected that they could defeat Lincoln in the election of 1864 over the issue of the emancipation of the slaves.

It is easy to skip over the word *"attributes."* It is not a word in popular use today. In Lincoln's day it was an important word in Old School Presbyterian circles. He now brought it into the Second Inaugural. Who was this God who *"gives to both North and South, this terrible war"*? Lincoln answered that question by observing that God's activity is no *"departure from those divine attributes which the believers in a Living God always ascribe to Him."*

The theological affirmation that Lincoln was making was that *"divine attributes"* presume and define a *"Living God."* In the Christian idea of providence, God is a personal, *"Living God"* who is the source of all life. Fatalism or determinism, on the other hand, was oriented around the depersonalization of the concept of God.

It can be argued that when Lincoln spoke of *"those divine attributes which the believers in a Living God always ascribe to Him"* he was describing belief in God, but not including himself in the circle of believers. In other words, he was using descriptive but not prescriptive language. I believe that his form of speech here is consistent with other examples of his rhetoric. When he ran for president in 1860, he spoke of himself in the third person in his campaign biographies. When he delivered his Second Inaugural Address, he used personal pronouns only in the first paragraph, and from there on directed all attention away from himself. Yet these forms of speech did not mean that Lincoln was not speaking from the vantage point of his own personal beliefs.

Most likely, Lincoln heard Gurley speak of *"divine attributes."* Any student of Hodge would have learned the language of *"attributes"* from the Princeton theologian. In volume 1 of his *Systematic Theology,* Hodge titled chapter 5 "The Nature and Attributes of God." He spent almost eighty pages making the case that these attributes are "essential to the nature of a divine Being."[36]

Of course, Hodge and Gurley were building on the language of attributes from the Westminster Confession of Faith. English-speaking Presbyterians had brought the Westminster Confession of Faith with them across the Atlantic at the beginning of the seventeenth century. The Westminster Confession functioned for Presbyterians in the United States as an authoritative interpretation of Biblical faith. The Westminster Shorter Catechism was a basis for Christian education in Presbyterian congregations. One of the sticking points in the Old School–New School split of 1837 was the Old School's determination to hold on tenaciously to the Westminster Confession in the face of theological innovation and revivalistic experience.

Chapter 2 of the Westminster Confession, surely familiar to Lincoln as a participant in two Old School Presbyterian congregations, began with a discussion of the attributes of God. God was defined at the outset as the "only living and true God," whose attributes included "gracious, merciful, long-suffering, abundant in goodness and love." At that same time, this God was "most just and terrible in his judgments."[37] The Westminster Confession of Faith spoke of a "living" God defined by both gracious action and terrible judgment. Lincoln, having sat in Old School Presbyterian congregations for more than twenty years, resorted to Old School language when he affirmed that *"believers"* would *"always ascribe"* certain *"attributes"* to God.

The important point is, finally, not the attributes themselves, but that these attributes presume that God is a personal being. A *"God"* who is *"Living"* has *"attributes,"* whereas fate does not. Behind Lincoln's words is the conviction that God is ordering human affairs because God is a *"Living God."*

Was Lincoln fobbing off upon God the responsibility for the incredible death and destruction of four years of war? In invoking God, was Lincoln calling down a *deus ex machina?* A *deus ex machina* was a god inserted, often by means of a crane, in ancient Greek and Roman drama, introduced in order to decide the final outcome. The problem with this solution was that it often appeared contrived.

Lincoln's solution was not contrived. For several years, he had been laboring to understand the great puzzle of the war, and brooding over the evil of slavery. If the rhythms of fatalism had been a comfort in the past, they were inadequate for the stormy present. A depersonalized God was not enough.

The logic and language of fatalism, important to Lincoln in his early and middle years, did not exhaust his thinking about historical causation. Under the enormous weight of war, Lincoln was forced to think more deeply about the historical basis of the war. In Washington, he found himself exposed to new sources that would push him beyond fatalism to an encounter with and appropriation of the ideas and language of providence.

Lincoln was not yet finished describing God's *"divine attributes."* The doctrine of providence has always been employed by preachers and politicians to invoke the special blessing of God on America. Lincoln was about to expand his definition of *"a Living God"* as he prepared to introduce the theme of judgment.

7

". . . every drop of blood drawn with the lash, shall be paid by another drawn with the sword . . ."

Fondly do we hope—fervently do we pray—that this mighty scourge of war may speedily pass away. Yet, if God wills that it continue, until all the wealth piled by the bond-man's two hundred and fifty years of unrequited toil shall be sunk, and until every drop of blood drawn with the lash, shall be paid by another drawn with the sword, as was said three thousand years ago, so still it must be said "the judgments of the Lord, are true and righteous altogether[.]"

As the address built toward its final paragraph, Lincoln made an unexpected political and rhetorical move. Speaking on the eve of military victory, when many expected him to celebrate the successes of the Union, he called upon his audience to recognize a perilous evil in their midst. Instead of self-congratulation, he asked his fellow citizens for self-analysis. No president, before or since, has so courageously pointed to a malady that resides at the very center of the American national family. Lincoln had come to believe that, where there was evil, judgment would surely follow.

As the war progressed, Lincoln had found himself struggling more and more with the recognition that evil traveled as a companion to the good. Now, at his inauguration for a second term, Lincoln surprised his audience by asking them to look at the malignancy of slavery that had been eating away at the heart of the American body politic. We can now understand that his chronicling of the events of war was actually his long look back at the ethical behavior of the nation.

Lincoln carried to his speech the scales of justice. He did so knowing that Americans had always been uncomfortable facing up to their own malevolence. We might think that the Civil War forced such an encounter, but evil in any war mostly seems to be relegated to the other side. Many in the North felt quite righteous in criticizing the South for rebellion and slavery. Most in the South believed they were acting in the spirit of the freedom of 1776 in severing ties with a tyrannical and hypocritical federal government. Now Lincoln concentrated a discussion on the problem of evil, weighed on the scales of divine justice.

———

If Lincoln enjoyed spoofing the sermons of frontier preachers as a young boy, the mature man employed a form of speech resembling sermons as old as the New England Puritans and as contemporary as the discourses of the evangelical abolitionists. In this section of the Second Inaugural, Lincoln contended with the American people because of the evil that he named the *"offence"* of slavery. His rhetoric here reminds us of a jeremiad.

The jeremiad became a powerful form of the sermon among the Puritans of New England. The name came from the lamentations of the prophet Jeremiah in the seventh century B.C.E. New England preachers in the last half of the seventeenth century lamented that their "city set upon a hill" was becoming corrupt. Puritan preachers sought a way to deal with this "backsliding" that was frustrating the discipleship of people who thought of themselves as "God's New Israel."[1]

Increasingly after 1660, the jeremiad became a characteristic Puritan utterance. It grew out of the conflict and consternation experienced by second and third generations entrusted with maintaining the vision of their forebears. These children and grandchildren, born in New England, found themselves caught between the original hopes of the founders and their own lived experience and practice. William Stoughton, in a sermon in April 1668, proclaimed, "What a sad Metamorphosis hath there of later years passed upon us in these Churches and Plantations." "O *New-England*," he continued, "thy God did expect better things from thee and thy Children."[2]

On designated fast-days, New Englanders assembled to hear such sermons. The thrust was that the people had sinned by straying from the original vision of their forefathers and thus deserved punishment. Their sin was linked with the judgment of God. Judgment should give rise to repentance. If there was repentance, the preacher offered the possibility of forgiveness. Forgiveness portended hope. Hope should lead to reform.

The meaning of the jeremiad was set within the Puritans' understanding of the covenant. On the one hand, Reformed theology accented the timeless truth that individuals were saved by grace alone. On the other hand, individuals were bonded together in a community based on a covenant with work to be done. God was the initiator of the covenant, but the responsibilities were understood to be reciprocal. The response to God's amazing grace was not passivity but activity. The elect of God were encouraged to perform a timely mission in the world. If the covenant of grace led individuals to heaven, the covenant community should lead to the transformation of society into a heaven on earth.

The employment of a jeremiad was always rooted in immediate difficulties. Betrayal of the covenant would not mean eternal judgment so much as present visitations of God's anger. The cause of God's displeasure related to specific events, such as drought or war; or behaviors, such as obstinacy or pride. The call was upon God "rather [to] correct us in mercy, then [sic] cast us off in displeasure, and scatter us in this Wildernesse."[3]

The jeremiad thus combined social criticism and reaffirmation. Various calamities became the occasion for the social criticism of an obstinate or refractory people. Facing up to these adversities became an opportunity to reaffirm the beliefs and behaviors associated with the founders of New England. The final purpose of the jeremiad was to encourage reform in the land.

The form of the jeremiad continued into the nineteenth century in different manifestations. The revivalism of the Second Great Awakening called people to repentance before calling them forward to the "anxious bench" where they could receive forgiveness and new life. Fiery abolitionists used jeremiads to condemn the sin of slavery and call for immediate abolition. The four fast-days that Lincoln proclaimed during the Civil War employed the same structure of the jeremiad.[4]

———

Lincoln's Second Inaugural resembled a jeremiad as he combined both criticism and reaffirmation. Because of the evil of the *"offence"* of slavery, the nation was deserving of God's indignation. The task of the preacher was to point out to the congregation the cause of God's anger. Slavery was the cause of God's wrath.

Lincoln's move to identify slavery as an *"offence"* to God shifted the balance of his address. Since 1854, all of Lincoln's major speeches had engaged the issue of slavery in predictable and consistent patterns. His major focus having been to block slavery's advance into new territories or states, he usually refrained from attacks on the horrors of slavery and exhibited no animosity toward Southern slaveholders.

But Lincoln resisted an attitude that had long repelled him. The abolitionists had focused on the evil of slavery resident in the South. Lincoln said there was blame that must be shared by the entire nation. The attitude of self-righteousness exhibited by some abolitionists not infrequently undermined their credibility. Lincoln, always sensitive to self-righteousness in any quarter, exhibited its direct opposite, magnanimity ready to cross any boundary to achieve reconciliation. If, for example, William Lloyd Garrison always seemed to put an "I" in front of his words, Lincoln pointed away from himself to "*'the judgments of the Lord.'*"

As in a jeremiad, Lincoln prosecuted his case not in generalities but with concrete visual representations. In a complex sentence of eighty-six words, he worked with imagery that brought the long dark night of slavery under an intense light that allowed his audience both to see and to understand the dimensions of this American "*offence.*" He used graphic descriptions.

"*Fondly do we hope—fervently do we pray*" conveys Lincoln's intensity of feeling. These invitations and petitions may sound a bit archaic to our ears. His words and tone reflected a kind of Victorian sentimentality that Lincoln enjoyed. "*Fondly*" and "*fervently*" also supported each other in alliteration. Lincoln allowed the force of his passions to resonate with what he knew to be the tensions in his audience.

Lincoln chose his words deliberately. He had heard Phineas D. Gurley use this same word "*scourge*" in exactly the same way in the sermon at the New York Avenue Presbyterian Church on the Sunday following the attack on Fort Sumter.

The meaning of "scourge" is "to chastise or punish." What the audience undoubtedly recognized was that "scourge" was often linked to the whipping a master inflicted upon a slave. A Biblically literate people would also associate "scourge" with divine chastisement. It is God who scourges.

Many in Lincoln's audience would have connected *"scourge"* with Hebrews 12:6, as rendered in the King James Version:

> For whom the Lord loveth he chasteneth,
> and scourgeth every son whom he receiveth.

Words change with fresh translations. Thus, the modern New Revised Standard Version translates this verse using the word "chastise" instead of "scourge."

> for the Lord disciplines those whom he loves,
> and chastises every child whom he accepts.

"Scourgeth," even to the contemporary ear, communicates a more intense action and feeling than "chastises." *"This mighty scourge of war"* conjured up the great and widespread affliction that would have affected almost every person in the audience that day.

Lincoln's depiction of the wages of slavery employed an earthy imagery. The initial figure conjured up the *"wealth"* produced by the labor of the *"bond-man,"* who himself reaped nothing of this wealth for his impoverished life. Lincoln used words full of grit. Even the enormity of this *"wealth"* that had been *"piled"* was now *"sunk."* The word *"toil"* portrayed the unrelenting, strenuous, fatiguing work of the slaves.

At the end of the day, this backbreaking work, rather than being rewarded, had instead gone *"unrequited."* As a young boy, Lincoln had resented his father for hiring him out to a neighbor for a day's labor and then expecting Abraham to turn over all his wages, forfeiting the reward for honest labor. It was not long before Lincoln's early belief in "the right to rise" collided with a system of slavery in which a hard day's work was not requited.

———

As Lincoln drew near the end of the Second Inaugural, his prose had the timbre and reverberation we associate with great poetry. We may speak of Lincoln's finest prose as a kind of poetry. The meter in Lincoln's words was never as consistent as it is in most poetry. It varied from regular to irregular. His language and style became more metrical as his words became more emotional.

Lincoln's writing resembled poetry in part because he was writing for the ear. Lincoln sometimes gave a primary accent to syllables that ordinarily would have received secondary stress. Listen to or say aloud the meter of these words, accenting the syllables in italics:

> *Fond*-ly / do we *hope*
> *Fer*-vent-ly / do we *pray*
> That this *migh-ty scourge* / of *war*
> May *speed*-i-ly pass / a-*way*

Liberties can be taken in poetry that one ordinarily would not take in prose.[5]

We also hear Lincoln's fondness for repetition and balance again. The Second Inaugural offers plentiful examples.

> *do we hope—do we pray*
> *drawn with the lash—drawn with the sword*
> *as was said—must be said*

I do not argue that Lincoln set out to write poetry. Yet he had a poet's ear.

———

As Lincoln examined the consequences of evil, he placed his judgments within two large historical contexts. In prosecuting the nation for the *"offence"* of slavery, he reached back beyond the nation's birth as he recalled *"two hundred and fifty years of unrequited toil."* Lincoln was reminding his audience that the stain of slavery had been enmeshed in the fabric of American history from its beginnings. In invoking *"'the judgments of the Lord,'"* Lincoln placed his remarks within the Psalmist's words uttered *"three thousand years ago."*[6]

Lincoln was asking the nation to recognize the war as the judgment of God for the *"offence"* of slavery. His sentiment paralleled William Stoughton's sermon two hundred years before. Behind Lincoln's words was a contention: "O America, thy God did expect better things from thee and thy Children."

Lincoln suggested that the war was a means of purging the nation of its sin. At the moment when victory celebrations were about to take place in New York, Chicago, and San Francisco, all would have welcomed some congratulations.

Some thought they heard Lincoln describing the conflict as a war of retribution. They had brought their own preconceived ideas about retribution toward the South. These ideas were expressed in 1864 presidential medals reading "A Foe to Traitors," and "No Compromise with Armed Rebels." Yes, there was mention of retribution, but this section on retribution and judgment would be a part of the address that was misunderstood, its meaning contested after Lincoln's death when cries for retribution against the South grew in number and volume. It was hard for many in the North to hear Lincoln arguing that the war was divine retribution aimed at both sides.

———

The images reach their zenith in

until every drop of blood drawn with the lash, shall be paid
by another drawn with the sword. . . .

Listening to this passage, one feels the anguish. His words sound here more like the romantic language of Harriet Beecher Stowe than the legal language of the lawyer who delivered the First Inaugural.

If a present-day president were to use such words, they would surely jar. But the people in Lincoln's audience lived close to the threat and reality of death, war, disease, and fire. For Lincoln, the image of blood was double-edged. First, the figure of blood pointed to two and a half centuries of the unfair and unacceptable burden borne by black American slaves who longed for freedom. Second, with wounded soldiers everywhere in the audience, his words spoke to the price borne by soldiers on both sides.

———

The sword of military battle was the judgment of God. Lincoln's confidence in *"'the judgments of the Lord'"* was drawn from the 19th Psalm. This was the fourth and final Biblical passage he quoted.

The judgments of the Lord, are true and righteous altogether.
[Psalm 19:9]

Although this line declares judgment, we need to read the entire psalm. If we look at it whole, we can understand the spirit in which Lincoln concluded this crucial paragraph. The Psalmist expressed confidence in a great and good God.

"The heavens are telling the glory of God, and the firmament showeth His handiwork." After speaking of the goodness of creation, the Psalmist shifts the focus to the Torah, or instruction. In the Hebrew Bible or Old Testament, "judgment" was often paired with "righteousness." Living by God's judgments constituted righteousness.

Certainly Lincoln believed that God had blessed America. His words that America was "the last, best, hope of earth," spoken as part of his second Annual Message to Congress, on December 1, 1862, spoke to its uniqueness. But even these words were part of a final paragraph in which he juxtaposed the potential for both honor and dishonor.

> Fellow-citizens, *we* cannot escape history. . . . The fiery trial through which we pass, will light us down, in honor or dishonor, to the latest generation. . . . In *giving* freedom to the *slave,* we *assure* freedom to the *free*—honorable alike in what we give, and what we preserve. We shall nobly save, or meanly lose, the last, best, hope of earth.[7]

Lincoln shared with his contemporaries a belief in the special destiny of America. Where he distinguished himself was in his willingness to confront its ambiguities. Brooding over the honor and dishonor in his nation's actions, he was unwilling to reduce political rhetoric to national self-congratulation.

———

Frederick Douglass, who stood in the crowd stretching out before Lincoln, was riveted by these two final sentences of the third paragraph. Douglass had been bitterly disappointed by Lincoln's First Inaugural Address. He may have taken some consolation in having played a role in Lincoln's subsequent education about slavery and race.[8]

Eight years younger than Lincoln, Douglass grew up as a slave in Tuckahoe and Baltimore, Maryland. After he experienced what he described as "a religious awakening" at thirteen, his passion for reading found its focus in the Bible. In 1838, Douglass escaped slavery traveling in disguise by train from Baltimore to Philadelphia. Then, settling as a laborer in New Bedford, Massachusetts, Douglass joined the abolitionist movement led by William Lloyd Garrison. From 1841 to 1847, he lectured in the North and in Great Britain. He broke with Garrison in 1847, embracing the tactics of political action and rejecting Garrison's reliance on moral suasion. Moving to Rochester, New York, Douglass began publishing his own abolitionist journal, *The North Star.* By the 1850s, Douglass had become the leading African-American spokesman, attacking slavery and advocating an expanded role in the North for free blacks.

Douglass broke with many abolitionists when he backed the nomination of Lincoln, whom he viewed initially as a radical Republican. During the presidential campaign in 1860, he was troubled that Lincoln opposed the extension of slavery rather than supporting the outright abolition of slavery. Lincoln's conciliatory First Inaugural disgusted him.[9]

Douglass began to change his mind about Lincoln when the president issued his Preliminary Emancipation Proclamation on September 22, 1862. One provision called for the arming of black troops. Douglass had encouraged this action since the beginning of the war and now praised Lincoln for a belated step forward. His youngest son, Charles, and his oldest son, Lewis, volunteered to serve in the famous 54th Massachusetts Regiment.

Widespread events in 1863, however, would indicate the depth of white prejudice in the North. Draft riots in New York City in July resulted in blacks' being beaten to death, their homes and churches burned. Douglass found also that the

Union Army treated black soldiers as inferiors. Major George L. Stearns, who was responsible for black recruitment, urged Douglass to lay his concerns before Lincoln.

Douglass traveled to Washington on August 10, 1863. To his surprise, within minutes after presenting his card to make his presence known, he was invited in to see the president. Douglass pressed upon Lincoln the need for more official recognition of black troops, including the vexing issue of unequal pay for blacks.

If Douglass was surprised at his quick invitation to see the president, he was more astonished by the tenor and content of their conversation. In a speech several months later in Philadelphia, he offered his impression of his first one-on-one meeting with Lincoln. "I never met with a man, who, on the first blush, impressed me more entirely with his sincerity, with his devotion to his country, and with his determination to save it at all hazards." Although Douglass was not in agreement with all of Lincoln's views, he decided he could work with him in promoting the role of black soldiers in the Union effort.[10]

As Douglass looked forward to the election of 1864, he regarded a crucial issue to be the enfranchisement of blacks in the South. Once again disappointed in Lincoln, he attacked the president's silence on this question. John Eaton, a key figure in work with the freedmen, reported Douglass's frustration to Lincoln. The president invited Douglass to the White House in the bleak summer days of August 1864.

On that August 19, Douglass found Lincoln in a melancholy mood. He invited Douglass to work with him on how to encourage slaves in areas still under Confederate control to escape to the Union lines. Douglass had come to believe that Lincoln's views on the moral evil of slavery were becoming more prominent in his conduct of the war.

The Douglass who listened to Lincoln in the crowd had

acted as a valued critic. He recorded his own sense of these meetings with the president, during which he became convinced of "the educating tendency of the conflict" upon Lincoln.[11] Now he listened on March 4, 1865, with both curiosity and hope.

———

Forty-two days later, on Saturday, April 15, Frederick Douglass stood among the crowds assembled at the Rochester City Hall for a public memorial service for President Lincoln, who had died that morning. He took a seat toward the back of the auditorium. He had not been invited to be part of the list of speakers that Mayor Daniel David Tompkins Moore had hastily assembled. After the scheduled speakers delivered their eulogies, first one and then other voices called for Douglass to speak. He went to the platform to offer his eulogy.

Douglass recalled words from Lincoln's Second Inaugural Address. He described "those memorable words—words which will live immortal in history, and be read with increasing admiration from age to age." He then went on to quote two sentences from the address.

> Fondly do we hope—fervently do we pray—that this mighty scourge of war may speedily pass away. Yet if God wills that it continue, until all the wealth piled by the bond-man's two hundred and fifty years of unrequited toil shall be sunk, and until every drop of blood drawn with the lash, shall be paid by another drawn with the sword, as was said three thousand years ago, so still it must be said "the judgments of the Lord are righteous altogether."

He spoke the words from memory.[12]

———

How did Lincoln speak these words? Were the words about God's judgments in history spoken with resignation? Were they spoken defiantly, to emphasize the retribution due an arrogant and self-righteous people? Or were they said in anguish?

I imagine that he spoke these words slowly. And sorrowfully. I believe that the final words in this paragraph, " '*the judgments of the Lord, are true and righteous altogether,*' " were spoken with quiet resolution. At the end of the third paragraph, Lincoln did not intend to be adversarial. Quite the opposite. Lincoln the lawyer, now in this moment become pastor to the nation, seemed willing to rest his case on *"the judgments of the Lord."*

But this was not Lincoln's last word. The president was now ready to move quickly from the past to the future, from judgment to hope.

8

"*With malice toward none; with charity for all . . .*"

With malice toward none; with charity for all; with firmness in the right, as God gives us to see the right, let us strive on to finish the work we are in; to bind up the nation's wounds; to care for him who shall have borne the battle, and for his widow, and his orphan—to do all which may achieve and cherish a just, and a lasting peace, among ourselves, and with all nations.

The first eight words of Lincoln's last paragraph proclaim a timeless promise of reconciliation.

With malice toward none; with charity for all . . .

Lincoln began his final exhortation by asking all of America to enter a new era, armed not with enmity but with forgiveness. These words immediately became the most memorable expressions of the Second Inaugural. Quickly, in the short weeks left before his assassination, *"With malice toward none; with charity for all"* became the watchwords written in newspapers, inscribed on badges. And after his assassination, they came to represent Lincoln's legacy to the nation. They would become some of our sacred words. Other words of his, from the Gettysburg Address—"of the people, by the people, for the people"—endure because they forever define America.[1] *"With malice toward none; with charity for all*" defined Lincoln's vision for a post–Civil War America.

As Lincoln began this final paragraph, he had been speaking for barely five minutes. Surely he would continue his discussion of the war and slavery. The audience was waiting for him to speak about his policy and plans for Reconstruction. But now, in an address filled with surprises, he turned briskly to his unexpected conclusion.

Lincoln must have trusted that by now he had forged a bond with his audience. Well aware of their feelings of both hope and despair, he was about to ask his listeners for acts of incredible compassion. He would summon them to overcome the barrier of race and the boundary of sectionalism and come together again in reconciliation.

———

The last paragraph consists of a long sentence of seventy-five words. In his punctuation Lincoln uses six commas, four semicolons, and one dash. Try this sentence today on any grammar check on a computer and it will set off all kinds of bells and whistles. Many biographers and historians have felt the need to correct Lincoln's punctuation, to make him conform to contemporary manuals of style.

I have chosen not to change Lincoln's punctuation. It is in keeping with the patterns of nineteenth-century usage. In another sense, Lincoln's punctuation, with its commas and semicolons, is a key to the way he spoke the words. Lincoln punctuated for the ear. Anyone who has ever read aloud words in a public gathering will recall that the audience will pause and take a breath after every six or seven words, regardless of the actual punctuation. Lincoln spoke only 105 or 110 words a minute, in part because he paused often for emphasis. He used punctuation as markers to cue himself.

Although Lincoln often crafted short sentences, some of his most memorable prose was rendered in long and complex sentences. The Gettysburg Address is remembered for its brevity—272 words. Yet Lincoln concluded that address with a long and complex sentence of eighty-two words:

> It is rather for us to be here dedicated to the great task remaining before us—that from these honored dead we take increased devotion to that cause for which they gave the last full measure of devotion—that we here highly resolve that these dead shall not have died in vain—that this nation, under God, shall have a new birth of freedom—and the government of the people, by the people, for the people, shall not perish from the earth.[2]

———

To appreciate the trajectory of the concluding words of Lincoln's Second Inaugural, we need to hear an unvoiced "therefore" as the first word of the final paragraph. When Lincoln's Second Inaugural is remembered, it is most often by quoting all or part of the final paragraph. Curiously, much description and analysis fails to connect this passage with the rest of the address. The last paragraph, powerful on its own terms, achieves its ultimate power only when it is understood as part of the whole cloth of Lincoln's ideas and rhetoric. This unvoiced "therefore" connects paragraphs one through three with the final one.

Here Lincoln offers an ethical imperative, a response to his earlier political and theological indicative declared in the first three paragraphs. The symmetry of the Second Inaugural rises from the close connections between indicative and imperative.

The indicative refers to the assertion of objective fact, and states a relation of objective fact between the subject and predicate. The imperative mood demands action and obedience. It speaks of the nature of duty.

In most Protestant sermons, the indicative and imperative formed a familiar rhetorical structure the audience had come to expect. In the Presbyterian sermons that Lincoln would have heard, the preacher would have spent the first three-quarters of the sermon reciting a grand indicative. The indicative was about what God had done. The minister might work with multiple scriptural texts, but several indicatives were frequently present. A first indicative was that God had brought the people out of captivity in Egypt. The Puritans used this indicative to understand themselves as God's new Israel. Blacks found in this story both consolation in suffering and a model for liberation.

A second indicative was that God had wrought deliverance from the captivity of sin in the life, death, and resurrection of Jesus Christ. The indicative pattern of Christ became the pattern for an imperative of selfless love and reconciliation. This second indicative was a frequent motif in Phineas Gurley's sermons.[3]

Lincoln's grand indicative was that God had been present in the midst of the Civil War. God's providence is the prism through which he carefully refracted the meaning of the war. Lincoln points beyond himself and his generals to God as the primary actor. His pre-inaugural musings, from the "Meditation on the Divine Will" to the letters to Eliza Gurney, and now the Second Inaugural are his attempt to see, through a mirror darkly, God's actions in the war.

An indicative usually included both grace and judgment. *"American slavery"* was the *"offence"* that was the basis for *"judgment."* Was there any grace in the Second Inaugural? The grace or good news is that *"the Almighty has His own purposes."* This *"Living God"* was bringing about renewal through the purification of human purposes. For Lincoln, in the intersection of his politics and theology, grace and judgment were never far from each other.

Convinced of God's activity, Lincoln would never speak about God in the language of triumphalism or jingoism. He was always suspicious of visiting church delegations or ministers who knew exactly when, where, and how God was on their side. He could not be comfortable with those voices in the surging evangelicalism of his day which seemed too familiar with the Almighty. Lincoln, who did not wear his faith on his sleeve, never spoke brashly about God.

The imperative in a sermon is always a response to the indicative. The "therefore," whether voiced or understood, is the tissue between what God has done and what men and women are to do. If Lincoln's final imperative was ethical in content, it was pastoral in tone. Lincoln located this imperative after the indicative because he knew that what he was asking might be too much to expect of those who had encountered such great losses. If the imperative in the last paragraph was shorn of this indicative, Lincoln's ethics would become simply platitudinous "ought"s and "should"s.

A congregation, knowing that the minister was coming to the end of a sermon, expected to hear not platitudes but the practical imperatives they were to carry out. Thus, Lincoln asked them

> *to bind up*
> *to care for*

He was quite specific about the objects of ethical duty:

> *him who shall have borne the battle,*
> *and for his widow,*
> *and his orphan*

———

Lincoln began this final paragraph by juxtaposing three quite different human attitudes. He used the connective conjunction *"with"* to hold them together.

> *With malice toward none;*
> *with charity for all;*
> *with firmness in the right*

The use of *"with"* keeps these three attitudes in balance.

This passage exhibits Lincoln's fondness for parallel arrangements. Such an arrangement also increased the rhythmic quality and balance of his prose. In this paragraph, the first three phrases exhibited a precise use of an identical metrical pattern.

One potential difficulty with this beginning for modern audiences is Lincoln's choice of words. The word *"malice"* is seldom used today and the word *"charity"* might better be replaced by another word if we wish to capture Lincoln's original intent. *"Malice"* and *"charity"* still work, because they succeed within the beauty and symmetry of Lincoln's prose. They will succeed even better if we step back and recover Lincoln's meaning.

"Malice" was not a new word in Lincoln's lexicon. It was one of those words he had learned through the crucible of war. Lincoln ran up against *"malice"* the first time he tried to inaugurate a policy of reconciliation in a Southern state. The initial opportunity occurred in Louisiana in 1862. Admiral David G. Farragut had captured New Orleans in April 1862. Lincoln hoped that Louisiana could become a loyal state and thus a showcase for reconstruction. Factionalism among different interest groups within the state frustrated this hope.

On July 28, 1862, Lincoln wrote to Cuthbert Bullitt, a

Unionist in New Orleans. Less than a year and a half into hostilities, Lincoln was besieged with criticism for his conduct of the war. In this letter to Bullitt one senses his frustration with the contradictory advice he was receiving. In the light of the opinions of so many persons with partisan ambitions, the final three sentences to Bullitt achieve their full meaning: "I shall do *all* I can to save the government, which is my sworn duty as well as my personal inclination. I shall do nothing in malice. What I deal with is too vast for malicious dealing."[4] Lincoln discovered that partisanship was not simply between North and South, but could be found within all of the seceding states of what was now the Confederate States of America. Almost three years before writing the Second Inaugural, Lincoln was keenly aware of the temptation for himself and those around him to act in *"malice."*

Malice is not simply evil; it is directed evil, the intent to harm other people. As the war moved toward its climax, Lincoln found himself being asked with more and more frequency how he would treat those in the South. Many of those who asked were quick to answer their own question. Here, at the beginning of his final paragraph, he began to answer the question: *"With malice toward none."*

The word that Lincoln chose to convey the opposite of *"malice"* was *"charity."* The problem is that today this word does not fully communicate Lincoln's intention; it has lost its earlier meaning and resonance.

The English word "charity" is derived both from the Latin word *caritas* and the Greek word in the New Testament *agape*. "Charity" is the word Lincoln would have read in the King James Version of the Bible. There were actually three main Greek words for love in the New Testament. The charity of which Lincoln speaks is *agape,* from the Greek verb *agapa-ein*, which refers to God's love for humanity. The same noun is used for love of our fellow human beings when this is an unselfish love that seeks only the well-being of the other.

Lincoln was fond of the word "charity" in a variety of contexts. Almost half the time he would speak of "christian charity," usually not capitalizing the adjective. In a "Fragment on Pro-Slavery Theology," he set up an opposition: "'Give to him that is needy' is the christian rule of charity; but 'Take from him that is needy' is the rule of slavery."[5]

The best-known example of *agape* as love between persons is found in the words of the Apostle Paul in 1 Corinthians 13:4–6:

> Love is patient; love is kind; love is not envious or boastful or arrogant or rude. It does not insist on its own way; it is not irritable or resentful; it does not rejoice in wrongdoing, but rejoices in the truth.   [New Revised Standard Version]

This explanation of love, like Lincoln's exposition in the Second Inaugural, achieves its theological and rhetorical power because Paul expounds not just what love is but also what love is not. Today the word "charity" sounds paternalistic. Over time it became associated with works of charity.

Lincoln was audacious in talking not simply about unselfish love among neighbors, but love between enemies. Lincoln was asking his hearers to go beyond the usual understanding of "charity."

We catch the expansiveness of Lincoln's vision if we pay attention to his use of the words *"none"* and *"all."* Lincoln's grammar of reconstruction was defined by his use of the objects of prepositions. The employment of *"none"* and *"all"* extends the ethic of his Second Inaugural to the whole of the nation. Lincoln was saying that there should be *"malice"* toward *"none"*—understood to be Confederate leaders, soldiers, or citizens. He reiterated his ethic in a positive form when he asked his listeners to practice *"charity for all."*

Except not everyone in the audience understood *"none"* and *"all."* The audience members heard Lincoln's words, but did not fully grasp their meaning. Why should they? His words were as a musical counterpoint to a symphony filled with blaring and harsh tones that were being conducted in the public square in the days leading up to the inaugural.

It is easy to skip over the third of Lincoln's *"with"* passages:

> *with firmness in the right, as God gives us to see the right*

This third and final imperative neither was printed on the silk ribbons of that day nor is much quoted in our day. Lincoln clearly meant that malice, charity, and firmness were to balance each other.

The emphasis of his extended third imperative is on *"the right."* The implied question is: What is right? Or how can we know what is right?

This line echoed the close of Lincoln's Cooper Union Address of February 1860. Lincoln had argued in New York that the nation's leaders must not be "frightened . . . by menaces of destruction to the Government nor of dungeons to ourselves." He concluded: "Let us have faith that right makes might, and in that faith, let us, to the end, dare to do our duty as we understand it."[6]

There is a crucial difference between the ending at Cooper Union and the Second Inaugural. At Cooper Union, Lincoln concluded with one angle of vision: "as we understand it." In the final paragraph of the Second Inaugural, Lincoln's angle of vision had changed: *"as God gives us to see the right."*

Lincoln answered the question he had been asking himself—how do we know what is right—by changing the grammatical subject of his trajectory. Lincoln believed God to be the main actor in the war—he urged, therefore, an ethical response of *"firmness in the right"*—the imperative.

At Cooper Union, before the war, Lincoln could say with courage that "right makes might," and that we need to "dare to do our duty." Now, at the end of the war, he was not nearly so sanguine about might and duty. If he had been humbled by the intractability of war, he was not at all naïve that the nation's duty in peace will be easy either to understand or to accomplish. God had not always been the subject in Lincoln's addresses, but in the ethical imperative with which he concluded the Second Inaugural he changed the indicative subject from "we" to *"God."*

———

Lincoln's encouragement to offer *"charity for all"* was spoken to an audience accustomed to calls for retribution. An event that spurred this talk was the "massacre" of over three hundred Union troops at Fort Pillow, Tennessee, on April 12, 1864. This "atrocity" shocked a North noisy with anger toward the South. The story of Fort Pillow became sensational news as reports were transmitted that most of the Union soldiers killed were black. Cries for wholesale revenge were sounded across the North. How would the president respond?

Six days later, as he spoke at the Sanitary Fair in Baltimore, Lincoln provided the answer. When he came to the end of his speech, he abruptly changed his tone. "A painful rumor, true I fear, has reached us of the massacre, by rebel forces, at Fort Pillow." Lincoln announced plans for a congressional investigation. With cries of retribution already in the air, Lincoln concluded forcefully, "It will be a matter of grave consideration in what exact course to apply the retribution; but in the supposed case, it must come." Lincoln plainly had malice and retribution on his mind.[7]

"Remember Fort Pillow" became watchwords for black soldiers as they fought in subsequent battles to redeem their murdered comrades. What is less known is a poignant story emerging out of Fort Pillow. Mary Elizabeth Wayt Booth, widow of the slain Fort Pillow white commander, traveled all the way from her home in Ohio to Washington to speak with Lincoln. Her concern for African-American widows and their children, and Lincoln's response to her suggestion, make a compelling story that embodies the words in this final paragraph: *"With malice toward none; with charity for all."*

Fort Pillow was a Union outpost on a stretch of the Mississippi River forty miles above Memphis. General Gideon J. Pillow built the fort in 1862 on a bluff more than three hundred feet high near the confluence of the Mississippi River and Cold Creek. Major Lionel F. Booth, a regular-army officer, was placed in command on March 28, 1864. Booth commanded 580 troops, of which 292 belonged to the 6th United States Colored Light Artillery and the 2nd United States Colored Light Artillery.[8]

Early on the morning of April 12, Fort Pillow was attacked by forces under the command of Confederate General Nathan Bedford Forrest. By 1864, Forrest had become a huge figure in the war, revered in the South and reviled in the North. Possessing no military education, he despised West Point dogma that called for holding one-third of one's forces in reserve. Forrest's military strategy was to attack—over and over—usually from several directions at the same time. He was a master of cavalry, using horses for lightning attacks to reach decisive points where his outnumbered troops could suddenly gain the advantage. Called the "wizard of the saddle," Forrest was reputed to have had twenty-nine horses shot out from under him. To General Sherman he was "that devil Forrest" who should be "hunted down and killed if it costs 10,000 lives and bankrupts the [national] treasury."[9]

As the Confederates began their assault on Fort Pillow, one of the first casualties was Major Booth, killed by a Confederate sharpshooter at 9 A.M. Usually outnumbered, this time Forrest had under his command nearly fifteen hundred Confederate troops. At 1:45 P.M., under a flag of truce, Forrest demanded unconditional surrender and promised that the Union soldiers would be treated as prisoners of war. If the demand were refused, Forrest would not be responsible for the fate of the defenders of the fort. After several delays, the Union forces, under the forged name of Major Booth, declared that they would not surrender.

What followed became the subject of controversy, not just for weeks, but for years. Union soldiers reported that, as the defenders of the fort were overwhelmed, the soldiers threw up their hands to surrender. At this point the story becomes confused. The surviving Union soldiers charged that the Confederate troops, disregarding the clear signs of surrender, proceeded to massacre the black soldiers. Forrest's own report to General Leonidas Polk on April 15 stated, "The river was dyed red with the blood of the slaughtered for 200 yards."[10]

To the defenders, the intention to kill all the black soldiers was clear. The Confederates denied this charge. It is a matter of dispute even whether General Forrest's troops had faced black Union soldiers before. Forrest is reported to have said that he wanted this action to be an example that would demonstrate to the Northern people that Southerners would not permit black soldiers to fight against them.

Lincoln was besieged with calls for retribution. On May 3, he asked his Cabinet "to give me in writing your opinion as to what course the government should take in the case." He received long and very different replies. Cabinet officers Seward, Chase, Stanton, and Welles argued that Confederate troops equal in number to the Union troops massacred should be held as hostages. They contended that the Southern soldiers should be killed if the Confederate government admitted the massacre. Cabinet officers Usher, Bates, and Blair advocated no retaliation against innocent hostages, but argued for orders to commanders in the field to execute the actual offenders.[11] The responses in the Cabinet mirrored the debate being argued across the nation.

On April 22, the Joint Congressional Committee on the Conduct of the War began public hearings. The completed report mixed fact-finding and propaganda. Forty thousand extra copies were printed to satisfy the public demand. The cries to execute Confederate prisoners in eye-for-eye reprisals grew.

It was in the midst of the hue and cry that Mrs. Booth traveled from Fort Pickering at Memphis to Fort Pillow to identify her husband's body for reburial. When she arrived at the fort, she encountered numerous wives of black soldiers who had come for the same purpose. Mrs. Booth was struck that white women and black women were united in grief at the death of their husbands. But one critical difference prompted her decision to speak to President Lincoln.

On May 19, three weeks after her visit to Fort Pillow, Lincoln received Mrs. Booth at the Executive Mansion. She had come to urge Lincoln not to forget the widows and children of the black soldiers who had fought and died at Fort Pillow. Mrs. Booth explained to Lincoln that marriage, as a legal contract, was not possible for blacks who were slaves. She insisted that these black women were married, no matter what Southern law or custom said. She asked Lincoln to make it possible for the black women to be assured of government pensions just as she would receive a pension for herself and her children.[12]

We have no record of Lincoln's words to her, but we do have a record of his actions. On that same day he wrote to Charles Sumner, Republican senator from Massachusetts. Sumner, an ardent abolitionist, had often been critical of Lincoln. Nevertheless, Lincoln thought well of Sumner and now asked the senator to take the initiative in translating Mrs. Booth's request into law. Lincoln wrote to Sumner, "She makes a point" that "widows and children *in* fact, of colored soldiers who fall in our service, be placed in law, the same as if their marriages were legal." Lincoln wanted Congress to assure that "they can have the benefit of the provisions made the widows & orphans of white soldiers."

After some considerable political maneuvering, black widows and orphans were included in a law passed by the House and Senate six weeks later, on July 2, 1864. Behind the scenes of official Washington, an individual act of compassion was translated into a statute embodying justice for all.[13] Lincoln's words, once again, had been tied to deeds.

> *To care for him who shall have borne the battle,*
> *and for his widow, and his orphan*

As Lincoln came to the end of his Second Inaugural, he spoke about *"the work we are in."* Having won a second term, and with the resolution of the war on the horizon, Lincoln was convinced that both he and the nation were at a new beginning. He understood *"the work we are in"* as a long-term project.

Because we often view Lincoln's life through the lens of his assassination, we are tempted to see the Second Inaugural as an ending. This emphasis is augmented by photographs of the president that reveal a man who had aged tremendously in four years. In addition, not long ago there was speculation, now put to rest, that Lincoln would have shortly died of Crohn's disease. He did indeed look like a man of stress and sorrows. The *Chicago Tribune,* a staunch supporter of Lincoln, commented, "Many who saw him at his inauguration . . . were painfully impressed with his gaunt, skeleton-like appearance."[14]

Nevertheless, Lincoln, and those who heard him that day, understood his Second Inaugural not as an ending but as a new beginning. Four years before, the nation had begun a dark night of the soul. Now, in the spring of 1865, it was nearly daylight. At this new dawning, Lincoln was the elected leader who would lead the nation into a new era.

The president was already thinking in the future tense. Early in the war, he had proposed a graduated emancipation for slavery to run until the year 1900. He could have run for a third term that would have allowed him to serve as president until 1873. Lincoln's final paragraph envisions living into an America far beyond the armistice that would end the hostilities.

In this final paragraph, Lincoln returned to the unifying language of the first paragraph. Here again he speaks of *"us," "us,"* and *"ourselves."*

> . . . *as God gives us to see the right,*
> > *let us strive on to finish the work we are in . . .*
> > *among ourselves, and with all nations.*

If in the first paragraph these plural pronouns pointed to a common complicity in the origins of the war, in this final paragraph they point to the actors of a reconciled nation. In the future, the nation's leaders, from every state, would sit together under the new iron dome of the Capitol.

―――

Lincoln ended his Second Inaugural Address with a coda of healing:

> *to bind up . . .*
>> *to care for . . .*
>>> *to do all which may achieve and cherish a just, and a*
>>>> *lasting peace, among ourselves, and with all nations*

Portraits of widows and orphans now balance the images of blood and swords.

Lincoln had defined the signposts toward winning the peace by achieving reconciliation. In this final paragraph, he declared that the true test of the aims of war would be how we now treated those who have been defeated. If enmity continued after hostilities ceased, the war would have been in vain.

These are no maudlin words crafted for emotional effect. The final paragraph is sublime. His words are directed to the tough, practical living actions that must replace retribution with *"charity."*

In this final paragraph, Lincoln offered the ultimate surprise. Instead of rallying his supporters, in the name of God, to support the war, he asked his listeners, quietly, to imitate the ways of God.

9

"... better than anything I have produced, but ... it is not immediately popular."

As Lincoln concluded his Second Inaugural Address, people were still arriving. He had spoken for only six to seven minutes. After a brief silence at the end of the address, artillery combined with cannonades of applause from the crowd. Lincoln bowed in acknowledgment of their acclamation.

Chief Justice Salmon P. Chase stepped forward. At that time, the oath was administered after the presidential address. At Lincoln's first inaugural, the chief justice had been the aged Roger Taney, forever to be identified with the Dred Scott Decision of 1857, which reaffirmed that slaves were property and that Congress was obliged to protect that property. Chase had been elevated to the office of chief justice by Lincoln. On this day, when irony would be heaped upon irony, the man who had sought to displace Lincoln as the candidate of the Republican Party in 1864 would administer the presidential oath of office.

Chase gestured to the clerk of the Supreme Court, who handed him a Bible. George Washington, who brought his own Bible to his first inauguration, had initiated this part of the ceremony. Lincoln placed his right hand on the page of the Bible open to Isaiah 5. Chase asked Lincoln to swear upon the Bible. Lincoln repeated the presidential oath after the chief justice.

Lincoln ended with an emphatic "So help me God." He bent down and kissed the Bible. The dignity and solemnity of the scene were in stark contrast to Vice-President Johnson's earlier unseemly demeanor. The inauguration was completed at seventeen minutes past twelve o'clock.[1]

Chief Justice Chase presented the Bible to Mrs. Lincoln. He pointed to the pencil-marked verses from Isaiah kissed by the president.

> None shall be weary nor stumble among them;
> none shall slumber nor sleep;
> Neither shall the girdle of their loins be loosed,
> nor the latchet of their shoes be broken.
> Whose arrows are sharp,
> And all their bows bent,
> their horses' hoofs shall be counted like flint,
> and their wheels like a whirlwind.
> [Isaiah 5:27–28, KJV]

Lincoln left the portico and went directly to the basement entrance of the Capitol, where his carriage awaited him. The president, with his young son Tad scrambling to get in at his side, was driven back to the White House. The houses along the route were lined with admirers waving handkerchiefs from windows and rooftops. Sharpshooters were plainly visible from many buildings. John Wilkes Booth sauntered back along the avenue.

———

How did the inaugural audience respond to the address? Fortunately, the correspondent for the *New York Herald* reported their reactions in detail. We are told that Lincoln's entire address produced only intermittent applause from the large audience, but for one notable exception. African Americans in the crowd offered a steady "bress de Lord" at the end of almost every sentence.[2]

Lincoln paused after the fourth sentence in the first paragraph,

> *The progress of our arms, upon which all else chiefly depends, is as well known to the public as to myself; and it is, I trust, reasonably satisfactory and encouraging to all.*

The *New York Herald* writer believed Lincoln expected a response. There was none.

The first cheer followed the next-to-last sentence of the second paragraph, when Lincoln declared, *"Both parties deprecated war; but one of them would <u>make</u> war rather than let the nation survive; and the other would <u>accept</u> war rather than let it perish."* The crowd did applaud when Lincoln, speaking about slavery at the beginning of the third paragraph, stated, *"All knew that this interest was, somehow, the cause of the war."* The *New York Herald* correspondent reported Lincoln's words from later in the third paragraph, *"It may seem strange that any men should dare to ask a just God's assistance in wringing their bread from the sweat of other men's faces,"* as a "satirical observation" which "caused a half laugh" from the audience.[3]

At that point, the address was less than half over. Remarkably, there would be no more audible response, apart from the steady "bress de Lord," for the almost four hundred words that remained in the address. Today, we are accustomed to having inaugural addresses interrupted by frequent applause. The reporter remarked that these few reactions "were the only marks of approbation until the close of the address." The reporter's puzzlement in his reporting of the audience's response is evident.[4]

———

In the ensuing days, men got together around cracker barrels in grocery stores in hundreds of towns to discuss what "Old Abe" had said in Washington. Women spoke across back gardens to offer their opinions of the president's words.

Early the next morning, Sunday, March 5, at 3 A.M., the Western Union finally connected the telegraph wires from New York to San Francisco. This achievement was hailed as opening up a direct and almost instant communication never before possible. Four years before, in March 1861, riders of the Pony Express had stuffed copies of Lincoln's First Inaugural into their saddle bags as they rode across plains and mountains to deliver the new president's words to Sacramento. Now, in March 1865, newspapers took advantage of this new link to print the text of the address, delaying editorial comment until the next edition. As the address was flashed by telegraph to newspapers across the country, ordinary citizens on farms, and in towns and cities around the nation, responded to what Lincoln had said and not said. Their reactions captured a remarkably mixed response.

One Pennsylvanian wrote his complaint to Simon Cameron, Lincoln's first secretary of war. "Lincoln's Inaugural, while the sentiments are noble, is one of the most awkwardly expressed documents I have ever read." A. B. Bradford added, "When he knew it would be read by millions all over the world, why under the heavens did he not make it a little more creditable to American scholarship." Perhaps Bradford knew of Seward's help with the First Inaugural, for now he wondered, "Why could not Mr. Seward have prepared the Inaugural so as to save it from the ridicule of a Sophomore in a British University."[5]

Frederick Douglass was an astute observer of the meaning of both the event and the address. "The whole proceeding was wonderfully quiet, earnest, and solemn." He agreed with the observations of the reporter for the *New York Herald,* but went further in describing the mood: "There was a leaden stillness about the crowd."[6] He believed he knew why. "The address sounded more like a sermon than a state paper." Reflecting on Lincoln's words, Douglass said that he "clapped my hands in gladness and thanksgiving at their utterance." But when he looked around, he "saw in the faces of many about me expressions of widely different emotion."[7]

Young Charles Francis Adams, Jr., was in the crowd that day. Adams counted two presidents, John Adams and John Quincy Adams, in his lineage. His father, Charles Francis Adams, had served as minister to England since 1861, deserving much credit for keeping England neutral during the Civil War. Young Adams had been commissioned as first lieutenant in the 1st Massachusetts Cavalry. His regiment fought at Antietam and Gettysburg. In July 1864, Adams had been given a lieutenant colonel's commission in the 5th Massachusetts Cavalry, an African-American regiment. He had been promoted to colonel in early 1865. Now he found himself in Washington, determined to witness Lincoln's second inauguration.

The twenty-nine-year-old Adams wrote to his father in London on Tuesday, March 7, "What do you think of the inaugural?," then offered his own estimation: "That rail-splitting lawyer is one of the wonders of the day. Once at Gettysburg and now again on a greater occasion he has shown a capacity for rising to the demands of the hour." Adams concluded, "This inaugural strikes me in its grand simplicity and directness as being for all time the historical keynote of this war."[8]

———

Lincoln's audience, even when standing in the same location, facing the west wing of the Capitol, was really standing in many different locations. Their social and political locations had much to do with how they heard the speech. Charles Francis Adams, Jr., age twenty-nine, and John Wilkes Booth, age twenty-six, young white men, stood in radically different political locations.

Listeners and readers responded differently. By far the largest response was to the first words of Lincoln's final paragraph, *"With malice toward none; with charity for all."* Those words were picked up immediately after the address in newspaper accounts and editorials. They were quickly fashioned upon badges, medals, and ribbons. After Lincoln's assassination, when there was a great outpouring of affection for the slain president, these words were frequently quoted.

Another response focused on Lincoln's words about slavery. Shortly after the Second Inaugural, Mrs. Amanda H. Hall wrote a letter to her brother, Thomas W. Ferry, a member of the House of Representatives from Michigan. Congressman Ferry showed the letter to Lincoln.

Lincoln, "induced by a letter of yours to your brother," wrote to Mrs. Hall on March 20, transcribing in his own hand these words from the Second Inaugural.

Fondly do we hope—fervently do we pray—that this mighty scourge of war may speedily pass away. Yet, if God wills that it continue, until all the wealth piled by the bond-man's two hundred and fifty years of unrequited toil shall be sunk, and until every drop of blood drawn with the lash, shall be paid by another drawn with the sword, as was said three thousand years ago, so still it must be said "the judgments of the Lord, are true and righteous altogether[.]"[9]

Mrs. Hall was drawn to the same passage that captured Frederick Douglass. Almost immediately, many facsimiles of Lincoln's words to her were produced. Years later, many owners believed that they had the original letter from Lincoln, because the facsimiles had the appearance of the original.[10]

———

Of course American newspapers weighed in with their responses. There had been an explosion of newspapers in the nineteenth century. In 1800, there were approximately 250 newspapers. By 1860, there were more than twenty-five hundred, both daily and weekly, more newspapers than the rest of the world combined. Some people read two, three, or four newspapers a day in their hunger to encounter a world beyond the farm, village, or small town.

As political participation increased with the growth of political parties, most newspapers became highly partisan. Their editorials and reporting reflected their respective positions. In large and even smaller cities one found newspapers with opposite political points of view.

During the Civil War, newspapers in the major cities conflicted dramatically regarding Lincoln as president. The *New York Times* and the *New York World* disagreed about Lincoln, the war, and slavery. The *Chicago Tribune* and the *Chicago Times* could be expected to take opposite positions on Lincoln, the Emancipation Proclamation, and the Second Inaugural Address. In Cincinnati, the *Daily Commercial* was pro-Lincoln, whereas the *Cincinnati Enquirer* was anti-Lincoln.[11]

To experience this divided attitude was nothing new for Lincoln. In his hometown of Springfield, the *Sangamo Journal,* which became the *Illinois Daily State Journal,* was unswerving in its support. Editor Edward L. Baker led the way in fighting "the fire in the rear," the opposition to the war in portions of the Northwest. On the other hand, the *Daily Illinois State Register,* the Democratic newspaper in Springfield, criticized Lincoln throughout his career. Editor Charles H. Lanphier, a Virginian, did not like one thing about Lincoln. He promoted the charge that Lincoln was a joker and not a thinker. When Lanphier left the paper in November 1863, the *Register* continued to smear Lincoln.[12]

Lincoln made the newspaper his political platform. He spoke about the power of printing in a lecture on "Discovery and Inventions" delivered in several places in Illinois in the winter of 1859. He offered his opinion on "certain inventions and discoveries" that were "of peculiar value" because "of their efficiency in facilitating all other inventions and discoveries." Although prizing speaking and writing, Lincoln especially trumpeted printing, which "gave ten thousand copies of any written matter, quite as cheaply as ten were given before." Lincoln homed in on the value of printing. "Consequently a thousand minds were brought into the field where there was but one before." He welcomed the interchange that newspapers promoted.[13]

The major players in the press and in politics were often the same persons. Henry J. Raymond, publisher of the *New York Times,* was chairman of the Republican National Committee and a Lincoln confidant. The *New York World* was established as a Republican newspaper in 1860, but it foundered under mismanagement and was taken over by Mayor Fernando Wood of New York City and August Belmont, a leading banker. Both were Democrats hostile to Lincoln. Under the direction of the young editor Manton Marble, the *World* led the radical opposition to Lincoln during the war. Yet another politician, Democratic Congressman Benjamin Wood, owned the *Daily News* in New York and used it to make mischief for Lincoln.[14]

No one would have been more interested in the response of the newspapers to the Second Inaugural than Lincoln himself. He had been fascinated by newspapers his whole life. When he was the postmaster in the village of New Salem, Lincoln read the newspapers before handing them out. In 1832, Lincoln announced his first candidacy for the Illinois Assembly through the *Sangamo Journal,* a staunchly Whig newspaper. After entering politics in the 1830s, he reported on the Illinois legislature for the *Sangamo Journal.* He liked to hang out at the newspaper shop. He signed up subscribers. He liked to spend his evenings at the newspaper's city room, helping his friend Baker, the editor, a graduate of Harvard Law School, with editorials. Lincoln even wrote letters to the editor under assumed names.

As president, Lincoln was known to have stepped outside the White House to ask a person walking by to send a corner newsboy to his front door with the latest newspaper. His law partner, Herndon, reported that what Lincoln chiefly read was newspapers. He continued to read newspapers in the White House, although "peruse" might be the better word for a president who was also the commander-in-chief, working long hours every day. In Lincoln's study in the White House there were usually three Washington newspapers: the *Daily Morning Chronicle,* the *National Republican,* and the *Evening Star.* Many editors sent their newspapers to Lincoln in hopes that he would read their editorials. John Nicolay and John Hay, Lincoln's secretaries, read countless newspapers and reported to their boss what they read.

Lincoln was appreciative yet wary of newspapers. Both newspaper editors and ministers were the targets of some of his best and most biting humor. Invited to inspect a newly invented repeating gun, the chief feature being a design to prevent the escape of gas, Lincoln remarked, "Well, I do believe this really does what it is represented to do. Now have any of you heard of any machine, or invention, for preventing the escape of gas from newspaper offices?"[15]

From no source did Lincoln receive more gas than from the "newspaper generals" of the North. They were free with advice and quick with criticism, from the opening crisis at Fort Sumter through the emancipation debate to discussion of terms for ending the war. The "newspaper generals" were headquartered in New York: Henry J. Raymond of the *New York Times,* James Gordon Bennett of the *New York Herald,* and Horace Greeley of the *New York Tribune.* The *Times* was strongly Republican. The *Herald,* with the largest circulation in the United States—probably over 130,000—was Democratic and began the war with a pro-Southern posture. It also sold its newspapers in Europe and thus was in a position to influence European thought about the conflict. Horace Greeley was no admirer of Lincoln while the president lived. Greeley said in August 1864 that Lincoln was already beaten, though he changed his tune in the fall and supported Lincoln's re-election. How would the newspaper generals and editors respond to Lincoln's Second Inaugural?

———

The responses of the leading newspapers, even after placing them on the political map, offer some surprises. The usually friendly *New York Times* expressed its disappointment. The *Times* surely spoke for many in complaining, "He makes no boasts of what he has done, or promises of what he will do. He does not reexpound the principles of the war; does not redeclare the worth of the Union; does not reproclaim that absolute submission to the Constitution is the only peace." The best praise the *New York Times* could offer was simply, "All that he does is simply to advert to the cause of the war;

and its amazing development; to recognize in the solemn language the righteous judgment of Heaven; and to drop an earnest exhortation that all will now stand by the right and strive for a peace that shall be just and lasting."[16] The *New York Times,* a supporter of Lincoln, was not very impressed.

The *New York Herald* was "disappointed" that Lincoln had said nothing about the recent Hampton Roads Peace Conference, for it "would have gratified loyal states." The *Herald* was even more disappointed in Lincoln's "silence" about such important topics as the Mexican question, Napoleon, Maximilian, and the Monroe Doctrine, to say nothing of the entire Baltimore Platform, "on which he was re-elected." The *Herald* opined, "Its main topic was slavery as the war cause." Lincoln accepted the war "as God punishing the nation for the 'offence' of slavery." Because Lincoln did not mention the Thirteenth Amendment, whose purpose was to abolish slavery by law, the *Herald* concluded that in the end Lincoln was solely dependent on the sword to abolish slavery. In this spirit the *Herald* reporter argued with Lincoln's peroration by stating that the intention to destroy slavery "contradicts Abraham Lincoln's call to 'charity for all.'"[17]

The *Herald* editorial had little good to say about the Second Inaugural, which it called "a little speech of 'glittering generalities' used only to fill in the program." It deemed Lincoln's remarks "not up to the mark of Napoleon's last imperial speech." Finally, the *Herald* complained that "the Second Inaugural address was an effort to avoid any commitment regarding our domestic or foreign affairs."[18]

The *World* editorial made the *Herald* look tame. "It is with a blush of shame and wounded pride, as American citizens, that we lay before our readers to-day the inaugural addresses of President Lincoln and Vice-President Johnson. But we cannot hide the dishonor done to the country we love by withholding these documents from publication." The *World* found Lincoln's words completely wanting, compared with what was needed at this hour of crisis. "The pity of it, that a divided nation should neither be sustained in this crisis of agony by words of wisdom nor cheered with words of hope."[19]

The *Chicago Times,* under editor Wilbur Fiske Storey, had opposed all forms of emancipation. As a copperhead or peace Democrat, Storey broke with Lincoln when the emancipation plan was first announced, in September 1862. The *Times* now offered this opinion of the Second Inaugural: "We did not conceive it possible that even Mr. Lincoln could produce a paper so slip shod, so loose-jointed, so puerile, not alone in literary construction, but in its ideas, its sentiments, its grasp."[20]

In Lincoln's hometown of Springfield, readers had long been accustomed to harangues from the *Daily Illinois State Register.* The editorial of March 8, under the title "Biblical Acumen and Presidential Prophecy," stated that the Second Inaugural was "not a very felicitous nor satisfactory performance." Declaring that many topics "were pressing upon public importance," the editorial complained, "our revered president should have neither time nor impulse to devote to them a moment's consideration." The *Register* acknowledged "our good opinion of his biblical learning," but used this applause as the opportunity to indict Lincoln: "He does not hesitate to pray into the arcana of God's council."[21]

The Philadelphia newspapers had put their trust in the president throughout his entire first term. All were Republican except the *Evening Journal.* Publisher Jesper Harding of the *Philadelphia Inquirer* had criticized the armchair generals of the New York press for their constant criticism of Lincoln. Harding had consistently backed the president's patient handling of the war.

It was no surprise that the *Philadelphia Inquirer*'s response to the Second Inaugural diverged from the opinion of the New York newspapers. "The address is characteristic of Mr. Lincoln. It exhibits afresh the kindness of his heart, and the large charity which has ever marked his actions toward those who are his personal enemies as well as enemies of his country."[22]

The *Washington (D.C.) Daily National Intelligencer* had been only lukewarm in its support of his administration under the editorship of William W. Seaton, an aging Virginian. Only months before Lincoln's second inauguration, there had been a change of ownership and an abrupt change of policy toward support for Lincoln. The *Intelligencer* concluded its editorial with acclaim for the words of the final paragraph. "They are equally distinguished for patriotism, statesmanship, and benevolence, and deserve to be printed in gold."[23]

The *Jersey City Times* believed the address might yet convert some of Lincoln's critics. "It will stand forever as an announcement, grand in its simplicity, and unflexible in its resolve, of the faith of the American people in the stability of their free government and the justice and invincibility of their cause." The ultimate praise was due the author of the address. "It will make thousands say, who have not hitherto said, 'God bless Abraham Lincoln.'"[24] The editorial predicted that the address would take its place in history.

In the South, Lincoln's Second Inaugural offered particular problems. The motto of the Confederacy, *Deo vindice* (God will avenge), spoke to the South's self-identity as a Christian nation. Southerners were keenly aware that their Confederate Constitution, unlike the silence of the federal Constitution, included "invoking the favor and guidance of Almighty God." Throughout the war, Southern politicians and pastors had comforted themselves that they were the true Christian people, as contrasted with the North, which they charged had been corrupted by liberalizing movements in theology and non-Christian immigrants. What, then, to make of Lincoln's Biblical words and theological language?

Only a few newspapers in the South offered their opinions of the Second Inaugural. By the spring of 1865, only twenty-two newspapers were still publishing in the South. The five newspapers in Richmond reached an audience far beyond the boundaries of the capital of the Confederacy. Those newspapers generally blended piety with politics. The exception was the *Richmond Examiner,* which by the middle of 1862 had begun to complain that no amount of piety could take the place of manly honor and moral courage. Editor John Moncure Daniel began to stress a secular "patriotism" different from what was espoused by most other newspapers in the South. The *Richmond Examiner* was not hospitable, therefore, to Lincoln's combining politics and religion in the Second Inaugural. "It reads like the tail of some old sermon, and seems to have no particular meaning of any kind, at least, if any meaning lurks in it we fail to perceive it."[25]

The Second Inaugural occurred just at the moment when Grant was besieging Petersburg, Virginia, on his way toward Richmond. The *Daily Express* of Petersburg had not taken the tack of the *Richmond Examiner* concerning the place of religion in the Confederacy. One hears in the editorial of March 9 puzzlement about Lincoln's words. "His allusions to Almighty Power and his citations from the scriptures might well become a Preacher of Righteousness. He seems to be thoroughly imbued with reverence for the Gospel of peace and with faith in Divine revelations." The writer was puzzled by Lincoln's words as evidenced in his conclusion. "We will refrain from expressing our opinion, saying with Lincoln, who borrowed the idea and most of the words from our Savior's Sermon on the Mount: 'Let us judge not, that we be not judged.' "[26]

Many of the newspapers noticed the unusual feature of the theological content of the address. The *Washington Daily National Intelligencer,* a new supporter of Lincoln, commented that, by invoking "religious views," Lincoln was likely to run afoul of those who advocated a strict separation of church and state in public discourse. Thus, in their prediction of response to the address, the *Intelligencer* stated that Lincoln might be subject "to that sort of criticism" by the press.[27]

The *Intelligencer* was on the mark. The *New York World* made an attack on Lincoln's use of religion the heart of its assault, comparing Lincoln's remarks to a late encyclical letter by Pope Pius IX. The *World* disparaged the Pope's intention of subordinating secular rule to spiritual authority as an attempt to replace the politics of the nineteenth century with the politics of the Middle Ages. However absurd in the eyes of the *World,* the Pope's words were at least intelligible. Not so Lincoln's intention or words. "The President's theology smacks as strong of the dark ages as does Pope Pius IX's politics." Arguing with Lincoln's premise about the *"offence"* of slavery, the *World* stated, "Mr. Lincoln expects our cause to succeed by the prevailing efficacy of our prayers when we are to hold up the negro to heaven as a token of our penitence for other men's sins." The editor certainly missed Lincoln's emphasis on the inclusivity of the nation's sins. Finally, the *World* indicted Lincoln for "abandoning all pretense of statesmanship . . . in this strange inaugural" by taking "refuge in piety."[28]

Lincoln's address was reviewed in London and in some of the other capitals of Europe. English newspapers, many of which had supported the Confederacy for much of the war, offered thoughtful comment. The *Times* of London, with a record of four years of pro-Confederate editorials, stated, "This short Inaugural speech reveals Abraham Lincoln's disposition and opinions more completely than many verbose compositions of his predecessors." The *Times* correspondent appreciated that Lincoln spoke "without any feeling of exhilaration at success or sanguine anticipation of coming prosperity."[29]

The London *Spectator* was eloquent in its praise of both Lincoln's character and the address. "Mr. Lincoln has persevered through all without ever giving way to anger, or despondency, or exultation, or popular arrogance, or sectarian fanaticism, or caste prejudice, visibly growing in force of character, in self-possession, and in magnanimity." The *Spectator* recalled that in 1861 the "village attorney" was scorned in England. Now "we can detect no longer the rude and illiterate mould of a village lawyer's thought, but find it replaced by a grasp of principle, a dignity of manner, and a solemnity of purpose which would have been unworthy neither of Hampden nor of Cromwell, while his gentleness and generosity of feeling towards his foes are almost greater than we should expect from either of them." The *Spectator,* using Biblical imagery, opined that Lincoln "seems destined to be one of those 'foolish things of the world' which are destined to confound the wise, one of those weak things which shall 'confound the things which are mighty.'"[30]

The *Saturday Review* began by contrasting Lincoln with the usual posture it had come to expect from its American cousin. "If it had been composed by any other prominent American politician, it would have been boastful, confident, and menacing." The *Saturday Review* found, "His unshaken purpose of continuing the war until it ends in victory assumes the form of resigned submission to the inscrutable decrees of a superior Power."[31]

John Bigelow, an officer at the United States Legation in Paris, wrote to Secretary of State Seward to report on the French response. "The President's inaugural has enjoyed a rare distinction for an American state paper of being correctly translated and almost universally copied here." Bigelow offered his opinion as to why the address was so well received. Its success was "less due to its brevity than to its almost inspired simplicity and Christian dignity." Bigelow sent along an article from the *Opinion Nationale* as an example of this kind of commendation.[32]

A reporter for the *Chicago Tribune* cabled a similar response from Paris on March 21. "The message of President Lincoln . . . has been received here with unmitigated satisfaction, its moderation of tone, its wise reticence with respect to the war, the absence of all boasting either as regards the glorious past or the hopeful future, its truthfulness, simplicity and reverential character" contributing to "the reception and respectful attention it so well deserves." This writer focused on the closing words of the final paragraph, usually overlooked by American newspapers.

> . . . *and a lasting peace, among ourselves, and with all nations.*

As an American correspondent in Paris, the *Chicago Tribune* writer said he had been "pestered" by many inquiries of what would happen when the war was over and "the American Union once more restored to its full strength." Many in France were worried in the spring of 1865 that the end of the war could be followed quickly by "the appearance of an American fleet of ironsides in the port of Havre, or a fleet of gunboats sailing up the Seine to take Paris!" It was in this context that the French public, both political and commercial, responded so positively to Lincoln's "concluding words of peace and good will to all nations."[33]

A most important commentator was the president himself. Lincoln expressed himself in a response to Thurlow Weed, the New York Republican boss who wrote him on that same March 4. Weed had written to commend Lincoln's March 2 reply to the Committee of Congress's notification to the president of his re-election. Weed had also mentioned the second inauguration earlier that day. Lincoln evidently misconstrued Weed's commendation as kind words about both "my little notification speech" and the inaugural address.

Lincoln answered Weed eleven days later, on March 15, offering his thoughts about his Second Inaugural. "I expect the latter to wear as well—perhaps better than anything I have produced." Lincoln then adds a fascinating caveat that reveals much about his own perception: "but I believe it is not immediately popular."[34]

What did Lincoln mean about the address's not being "immediately popular"? He had read a variety of newspapers, as he always did, and so had read the mixed reviews and editorial comment. I think he had considered the risk in preparing his Second Inaugural, and understood before he delivered it that it would disappoint many people for various reasons. He surely knew that most people expected him to talk about policy and plans. Others might be put off by his extensive quotations from the Bible and his use of theological arguments and language. But the Whig and now the Republican parties had always tried to seize the religious high ground in their approach to politics.

Lincoln supplied his own answer. "Men are not flattered

by being shown that there has been a difference of purpose between the Almighty and them." Human purpose, whether of the North or the South, lay in the invoking of a tribal God. His purpose had been to invoke a universal God. He had dared to say that this God was judging the whole nation for the *"offence"* of slavery. With God there is no partiality.

The issue was, finally, one of purpose. "To deny it, however, in this case, is to deny that there is a God governing the world." He had pondered God's purpose in the "Meditation on the Divine Will" and come to the conclusion, "In the present civil war it is quite possible that God's purpose is something different from the purpose of either party." In his first letter to Eliza Gurney, he had linked this purpose to God's governing in the world. "We must believe that He permits it [the war] for some wise purpose of his own, mysterious and unknown to us; and though with our limited understandings we may not be able to comprehend it, yet we cannot but believe, that he who made the world still governs it."[35]

Lincoln's comments to Weed illuminate his own understanding of the text. His words underscore that in his mind the central theme of the address was *"The Almighty has His own purposes."* His beliefs had unquestionably moved far beyond any doctrine of necessity or environmental determinism.

Two thousand people crowded the streets outside the White House waiting for the inaugural reception. At eight o'clock, the gates were opened and the free-for-all began. Maggie Lindsley and her family attempted to attend the White House reception but could not even get inside the gates, "so great was the crowd!" William H. Crook, Lincoln's bodyguard, observed, "The White House looked as if a regiment of rebel troops had been quartered there—with permission to forage." In the East Room, Lincoln, looking slightly ill, prepared to shake the hands of the more than six thousand people who crowded the reception.[36]

One person in the afternoon audience was determined to attend the inauguration reception that evening at the White House. Arriving at 1600 Pennsylvania Avenue, Frederick Douglass found himself barred at the door by two policemen. When he protested, they informed him that their "directions were to admit no one of color." Douglass quickly replied that there must be some mistake, for "no such order could have emanated from President Lincoln." Whether there were any directions from anyone, or whether they were simply following precedent, we do not know. Perhaps to end the confrontation, which was blocking the entrance, one of the officers offered to escort Douglass in. Before long, however, Douglass found himself being escorted out a window that had been set up as a temporary exit because there were so many visitors. Douglass saw the trick and asked a passing guest to tell Mr. Lincoln that he was being detained. The appeal reached the president.

All of the handshaking stopped as Douglass entered the East Room. As he approached, Lincoln called out, "Here comes my friend Douglass." Douglass was certain that Lincoln's greeting was said in such a voice "that all around could hear him." Taking Douglass by the hand, the president said, "I am glad to see you. I saw you in the crowd today, listening to my inaugural address; how did you like it?"

Douglass responded, "Mr. Lincoln, I must not detain you with my poor opinion, when there are thousands waiting to shake hands with you."

"No, no," Lincoln answered, "you must stop a little Douglass; there is no man in the country whose opinion I value more than yours. I want to know what you think of it?"

"Mr. Lincoln, that was a sacred effort," Douglass replied.[37]

Epilogue

Forty-one days after delivering the Second Inaugural Address, Lincoln was dead.

Events moved quickly following the inauguration. In little more than a month, on April 9, 1865, Lee surrendered to Grant at Appomattox Courthouse, Virginia. The next day, official news of the surrender touched off tumultuous celebrations in Washington. On Friday, April 14, the Stars and Stripes was hoisted at Fort Sumter, four years to the day after their lowering had signaled the beginning of the war.

On the evening of April 14—Good Friday—while watching a play at Ford's Theatre, Lincoln was shot by John Wilkes Booth. He died the next day at 7:22 A.M. A stunned nation struggled to grasp the first assassination of an American president. On April 16—Easter Sunday—people in churches across the country hailed the martyred Lincoln as a savior who in his death shed his blood as an atonement for the sins of the nation.

Abraham Lincoln considered his Second Inaugural Address to be his greatest speech! With his death, the words of the Second Inaugural quickly took on new meaning. It now represented the central part of Lincoln's unfinished legacy. As people looked back to that brisk March day, Lincoln's words were understood as his last will and testament to America. The religious cast of the Second Inaugural gave it a power and authority that were singular. The address would be printed in various forms. His concluding words, *"With malice toward none; with charity for all,"* usually disembodied from the speech as a whole, came to characterize Lincoln for all time.

Our focus has been on Lincoln's words. But in the end, Lincoln's rhetoric is Lincoln himself. No analysis of technique can fully explain the deep, brooding spirit that underlies his words. To trace his development as an artist is to trace his growth into greatness.

When leadership and integrity seem in short supply, Lincoln has emerged again into our national consciousness. Whereas many famous eighteenth- or nineteenth-century leaders or writers seem confined to the past, Lincoln and his words stride across the centuries with the capacity to both convict and to heal.

If Lincoln is remembered for leading the nation through war, we must not miss the battle within himself. He had prevaricated in the struggle over slavery. As president, he had been pressured and criticized by both friend and foe about the question of emancipation. Now, by the spring of 1865, he had come to some peace within himself as he looked forward to leading a nation into peace. At the Second Inaugural, not knowing he is going to die, his words sum up the life and thought of the man whom future generations esteem as the greatest American.

For too long the Second Inaugural Address has lived within the shadow of the Gettysburg Address. The Second Inaugural is paired with the Gettysburg Address in the templed space of the Lincoln Memorial. Millions upon millions of visitors have ascended the steps of the Lincoln Memorial, arrived at Daniel C. French's grand statue of Lincoln, and turned to their right to encounter the words of Lincoln's Second Inaugural Address carved in the Indiana limestone of the North interior wall.

The spirit of Lincoln's words inspires awe. His words prove lasting because he embodied what he spoke. He acted throughout his presidency *"with malice toward none; with charity toward all."* Still, awe is not to be confused with sentimentality.

Neither vindication nor triumphalism is present in the Second Inaugural. At the bedrock is Lincoln's humility. He included himself as one who *"looked for an easier triumph, and a result less fundamental and astounding."* As Lincoln told Thurlow Weed on March 15, "Whatever of humiliation there is in it, falls most directly on myself."[1] We might wish that Lincoln had expanded upon this reflection, but surely he meant that he did not claim for himself moral high ground in the nation's struggle with the immorality of slavery.

The Lincoln that is available to us comes with no simple answers. The chasm of race, which undergirded the legal structure of slavery, continues even though the Civil Rights movement, a hundred years after the Civil War, spearheaded political and legal action intended to right ancient wrongs. Martin Luther King, Jr., chose to speak with the imposing statue of Lincoln as the background when he offered his dream for America.

Lincoln is present to us in his own agonizing struggle for justice and reconciliation. He encourages us to ask difficult questions as we accept responsibility for defining America in our time. Lincoln offers little comfort for those who in every crisis or war want to chant, "God is on our side."

The separation of church and state in the United States has never meant the separation of religion and politics. In words that surprised his audience, Lincoln brought to his address deep theological thinking and argument. But even as he grounds his argument with Biblical moorings, Lincoln speaks forever against any "God bless America" theology that fails to come to terms with evil and hypocrisy in its own house. While the audience waited to hear words of self-congratulation, Lincoln continued to explain the implications of the judgment of God. He knew that the peril of theological politics is the danger of self-righteousness.

Lincoln wrote for all time. Overwhelmed by the decisions and the death toll of the Civil War, Lincoln saw that the issues at hand would not be solved by either emancipation or armistice. As the war drew to a close, Lincoln offered his sermon as the prism through which he himself strained to see the light of God. The refractions from that prism point to judgment and hope.

Appendix I:

The Text of the Second Inaugural Address

The text is shown two times. The first is a copy of the text in Lincoln's hand. The original is at the Library of Congress.

On April 10, the president gave the original text to one of his secretaries, John Hay. At the bottom of the address was added:

Original manuscript of second Inaugeral [sic] presented to

Major John Hay
April 10, 1865   A. Lincoln

Mr. Hay's children presented it to the Library of Congress in 1916.

The second is the text printed in a typeset version at the front of the book. We have no knowledge of any other primary text, nor do we have information about any editors. Lincoln made three corrections to the text.

1. In the opening sentence of the third paragraph, Lincoln was speaking about the distribution of the slaves. He changed the final phrase from *"in the Southern half of it"* to *"in the Southern part of it."* The significance of this change is discussed in chapter 4.

2. In the fourth paragraph, Lincoln changed *"four thousand years ago"* to *"three thousand years ago."* The changing of the number does not diminish the point he was making. Again, see the discussion in chapter 4.

3. The final correction occurred in the final sentence of the last paragraph. Lincoln changed *"and with all the world"* to *"and with all nations."* I take this to be a rhetorical change. The substance of the idea is not altered, but the change sounds and reads better.

If you look closely at the text, you will also be able to find what are either slips of the pen or slips in spelling. In the first paragraph, the third sentence reads *"enerergies"* instead of *"energies."* In the second paragraph, there are two errors in the third sentence. Lincoln misspelled *"inaugural."* (He made the same error in endorsing the gift to John Hay. Among some of Lincoln's friends he did not enjoy the reputation of a precise speller.) In the same sentence, he wrote *"dissole"* instead of *"dissolve."* Lincoln also practiced what today would be deemed peculiarities of capitalization and punctuation. Some of what we might consider errors were patterns practiced in the middle of the nineteenth century. None of them depreciate the quality or style of the text as a whole.

APPENDIX II

Lincoln's "Little Speech": Letter to Albert G. Hodges

A. G. Hodges, Esq
Frankfort, Ky.

Executive Mansion
Washington, April 4, 1864

My dear Sir: You ask me to put in writing the substance of what I verbally said the other day, in your presence, to Governor Bramlette and Senator Dixon. It was about as follows:

"I am naturally anti-slavery. If slavery is not wrong, nothing is wrong. I can not remember when I did not so think, and feel. And yet I have never understood that the Presidency conferred upon me an unrestricted right to act officially upon this judgment and feeling. It was in the oath I took that I would, to the best of my ability, preserve, protect, and defend the Constitution of the United States. I could not take the office without taking the oath. Nor was it my view that I might take an oath to get power, and break the oath in using the power. I understood, too, that in ordinary civil administration this oath even forbade me to practically indulge my primary abstract judgment on the moral question of slavery. I had publicly declared this many times, and in many ways. And I aver that, to this day, I have done no official act in mere deference to my abstract judgment and feeling on slavery. I did understand, however, that my oath to preserve the constitution to the best of my ability, imposed upon me the duty of preserving, by every indispensable means, that government—that nation—of which that constitution was the organic law. Was it possible to lose the nation, and yet preserve the constitution? By general law life *and* limb must be protected; yet often a limb must be amputated to save a life; but a life is never wisely given to save a limb. I felt that measures, otherwise, unconstitutional, might become lawful, by becoming indispensable to the preservation of the constitution, through the preservation of the nation. Right or wrong, I assumed this ground, and now avow it. I could not feel that, to the best of my ability, I have even tried to preserve the constitution, if, to save slavery, or any minor matter, I should permit the wreck of government, country, and Constitution all together. When, early in the war, Gen. Fremont attempted military emancipation, I forbade it, because I did not then think it an indispensable necessity. When a little later, Gen. Cameron, then Secretary of War, suggested the arming of blacks, I objected, because I did not think it an indispensable necessity. When, still later, Gen. Hunter attempted military emancipation, I again forbade it, because I did not yet think the indispensable necessity had come. When, in March, and May, and July 1862 I made earnest, and successive appeals to the border states to favor compensated emancipation, I believed the indispensable necessity for military emancipation, and arming the blacks would come, unless averted by that measure. They declined the proposition; and I was, in my best judgment, driven to the alternative of either surrendering the Union, and with it, the Constitution, or of laying strong hand upon the colored element. I chose the latter. In choosing it, I hoped for greater gain than loss; but of this, I was not entirely confident. More than a year of trial now shows no loss by it in our foreign relations, none in our home popular sentiment, none in our white military force,—no loss by it any how or any where. On the contrary, it shows a gain of quite a hundred and thirty thousand soldiers, seamen, and laborers. These are palpable facts, about which, as facts, there can be no caviling. We have the men; and we could not have had them without the measure.

["]And now let any Union man who complains of the measure, test himself by writing down in one line that he is for subduing the rebellion by force of arms; and in the next, that he is for taking these hundred and thirty thousand men from the Union side, and placing them where they would be but for the measure he condemns. If he can not face his case so stated, it is only because he can not face the truth.["]

I add a word which was not in the verbal conversation. In telling this tale I attempt no complement to my own sagacity. I claim not to have controlled events, but confess plainly that events have controlled me. Now, at the end of three years struggle the nation's condition is not what either party, or any man devised, or expected. God alone can claim it. Whither it is tending seems plain. If God now wills the removal of a great wrong, and wills also that we of the North as well as you of the South, shall pay fairly for our complicity in that wrong, impartial history will find therein new cause to attest and revere the justice and goodness of God. Yours truly.

A. Lincoln[1]

APPENDIX III

Abraham Lincoln:
"Meditation on the Divine Will"

September 2 [?], 1862

Lincoln wrote this private musing in September 1862. His young secretary, John Hay, found this text after Lincoln's death. Hay gave it the title "Meditation on the Divine Will" in 1872. Lincoln did not give a date to this rumination. Hay and Nicolay gave the date of September 30, 1862, to the "Meditation" in their *Complete Works* (vol. 8, p. 52). They associated the "Meditation" with Lincoln's struggles over issuing the Emancipation Proclamation. Roy P. Basler and the editors of *The Collected Works of Abraham Lincoln* suggest that the meditation was written earlier, on September 2, 1862, after Lincoln learned of the disastrous Union defeat at the Second Battle of Bull Run.

the cause of the conflict might cease w[ith] even before, the conflict itself should cea[se] looked for an easier triumph, and a resul[t] fundamental and astounding. Both read [the] Bible, and pray to the same God; and e[ach] vokes His aid against the other. It may [seem] strange that any men should dare to as[k] God's assistance in wringing their brea[d from] the sweat of other men's faces; but let [us judge] not that we be not judged. The pray[er of]

The will of God prevails. In great contests each party claims to act in accordance with the will of God. Both may be, and one must be wrong. God can not be for, and against the same thing at the same time. In the present civil war it is quite possible that God's purpose is something different from the purpose of either party—and yet the human instrumentalities, working just as they do, are of the best adaptation to effect His purpose. I am almost ready to say this is probably true—that God wills this contest, and wills that it shall not end yet. By his mere quiet power, on the minds of the now contestants, He could have either saved or destroyed the Union without a human contest. Yet the contest began. And having begun He could give the final victory to either side any day. Yet the contest proceeds.[1]

NOTES

CHAPTER 1: INAUGURATION DAY

1. The detailed descriptions of different aspects of the inaugural week are taken from the accounts in numerous newspapers. The newspapers of this era were intensely political, often serving as political organs for parties or elements within parties. Their partisan points of view have been taken into account in constructing the context.
2. In Lincoln's time, the old Congress ended on March 4, the date of his inauguration, but a new Congress did not convene until December.
3. *New York Times,* March 4, 1865, p. 4; *New York Herald,* March 3, 1856, p. 5.
4. *New York World,* March 3, 1865, p. 4.
5. Philip S. Paludan, *"A People's Contest": The Union and the Civil War, 1861–1865* (New York: Harper & Row, 1988), p. 317, puts a human face on the Civil War statistics.
6. *Washington (D.C.) Daily National Intelligencer,* March 4, 1865, p. 3.
7. *New York Times,* March 3, 1865, p. 3.
8. *New-York Daily Tribune,* March 1, 1865, p. 1; March 6, 1865, p. 5; *New York Herald,* March 1, 1865, p. 4; March 3, 1865, p. 1.
9. *Illinois Daily State Journal,* March 4, 1865, p. 2.
10. *Chicago Tribune,* March 3, 1865, p. 2.
11. *Washington (D.C.) Daily Morning Chronicle*, March 4, 1865, p. 2.
12. Charles Dickens, *American Notes* (London: Chapman and Hall, 1842), p. 45.
13. *Philadelphia Inquirer,* March 6, 1865, p. 3.
14. *New York Times,* March 3, 1865, p. 4.
15. *Times* (London), March 20, 1865, p. 9.

16. *Philadelphia Inquirer,* March 6, 1865.

17. Seldon Connor to Mother, March 6, 1865, Seldon Connor Correspondence, Lincoln Collection, John Hay Library, Brown University, Providence, R.I.

18. Maggie Lindsley, *Maggie Lindsley's Journal* (n.p.: privately printed, 1977), p. 73.

19. Dispatch to *Sacramento Daily Union,* March 12, 1865 (published April 10), in *Lincoln Observed: Civil War Dispatches of Noah Brooks,* ed. Michael Burlingame (Baltimore: Johns Hopkins University Press, 1998), p. 165. Noah Brooks's memoir, based on his dispatches, *Washington in Lincoln's Time* (New York: Century, 1896), p. 210, sometimes omits the more detailed and colorful language of the original reports.

20. *New York Herald,* March 6, 1865, p. 5.

21. *Times (*London), March 20, 1865, p. 9 (report, "From Our Correspondent," written March 7); *New York Herald,* March 6, 1865, p. 4.

22. *New York Tribune,* March 5, 1865.

23. William C. Allen, *The Dome of the United States Capitol: An Architectural History* (Washington, D.C.: Government Printing Office, 1992), p. 17.

24. Ibid., p. 55.

25. Ibid., p. 57. Allen, the architectural historian to the architect of the Capitol, states, "Lincoln's shrewd political skill may be credited for turning the contractor's decision into a symbol of national resolve."

26. Jefferson Davis to Montgomery C. Meigs, January 15, 1856, quoted in ibid., p. 42. Sometimes the statue has been called "Freedom."

27. Ibid., p. 60.

28. Roger A. Fischer, *Tippecanoe and Trinkets Too: The Material Culture of American Presidential Campaigns, 1828–1984* (Urbana: University of Illinois Press, 1988), pp. 94–96.

29. *New York Herald,* March 6, 1865, p. 5.

30. The account of Johnson's maudlin performance, which aroused such disgust, is in Hans L. Trefousse, *Andrew Johnson: A Biography* (New York: W. W. Norton, 1989), pp. 188–90.

31. Gideon Welles, *Diary of Gideon Welles, Secretary of the Navy Under Lincoln and Johnson* (Boston: Houghton Mifflin, 1911), vol. 2, p. 252.

32. *New York Herald,* March 6, 1865.

33. George Fort Milton, *The Age of Hate: Andrew Johnson and the Radicals* (New York: Coward-McCann, 1930), p. 147.

34. Brooks, *Washington in Lincoln's Time,* p. 212.

35. Waldo E. Martin Jr., *The Mind of Frederick Douglass* (Chapel Hill: University of North Carolina Press, 1984), pp. 63–64.

36. Brooks, *Washington in Lincoln's Time,* p. 213.

37. Benjamin Brown French, *Witness to the Young Republic: A Yankee's Journal, 1828–1870* (Hanover, N.H.: University Press of New England, 1989), Dec. 12, 1864, pp. 460–61; Allen, *Dome of the Capitol,* p. 18. French ultimately gave the table to the Massachusetts Historical Society.

38. Michael Shiner, *Diary, 1813–1865,* Library of Congress, p. 182; Brooks, *Washington in Lincoln's Time,* p. 213.

CHAPTER 2: "AT THIS SECOND APPEARING . . ."

1. *New York Herald,* March 4, 1865, p. 4; *Times* (London), March 17, 1865, p. 9.

2. *New York Herald,* March 4, 1865, p. 4.

3. Raymond's letter is quoted in *The Collected Works of Abraham Lincoln,* ed. Roy S. Basler (New Brunswick, N.J.: Rutgers University Press, 1953) [hereinafter cited as *CW*], vol. 7, pp. 517–18; see also Francis Brown, *Raymond of the Times* (New York: W. W. Norton, 1951), p. 260.

4. *CW,* vol. 7, p. 518.

5. Abraham Lincoln, "Memorandum Concerning His Probable Failure of Re-election," Aug. 23, 1864, in *CW,* vol. 7, pp. 514–15.

6. Francis B. Carpenter, *The Inner Life of Abraham Lincoln: Six Months at the White House* (New York: Hurd and Houghton, 1874), p. 234. Carpenter became famous for his historical painting *First Reading of the Emancipation Proclamation.*

7. Noah Brooks, "Personal Reminiscences of Lincoln," *Scribner's Monthly,* vol. 15 (Feb. 1878), pp. 565–66.

8. Harold Bloom, *Poetry and Repression* (New Haven: Yale University Press, 1976), p. 1.

9. In the following paragraphs I am indebted to insights from the rhetorical analysis in Michael Leff, "Dimensions of Temporality in Lincoln's Second Inaugural," in *Readings in Rhetorical Criticism,* ed. Carl R. Burgchardt (State College, Pa.: Strata Publications, 1995), pp. 526–31.

10. Thomas Jefferson, "Second Inaugural Address," March 4, 1805, in *Inaugural Addresses of the Presidents of the United States from George Washington 1789 to John F. Kennedy 1961* (Washington, D.C.: Government Printing Office, 1961), p. 17.

11. James Madison, "Second Inaugural Address," March 4, 1813, in ibid., p. 26.
12. James Monroe, "Second Inaugural Address," March 4, 1821, in ibid., p. 37.
13. Andrew Jackson, "Second Inaugural Address," March 4, 1833, in ibid., p. 58.
14. Franklin D. Roosevelt, "Second Inaugural Address," January 20, 1937, in ibid., p. 240.
15. The campaign that Roosevelt should appear for posterity with his paralysis no longer shielded from view ultimately won.
16. To take a look at the way Lincoln appeared in popular print, see two volumes by Harold Holzer, Gabor S. Boritt, and Mark E. Neely Jr., *The Lincoln Image: Abraham Lincoln and the Popular Print* (New York: Scribner, 1984), and *Changing the Lincoln Image* (Fort Wayne, Ind.: Louis A. Warren Lincoln Library and Museum, 1985).
17. Robert S. Harper, *Lincoln and the Press* (New York: McGraw Hill, 1951), pp. 92–93. This article, author unnamed, was reprinted in *The Crisis,* a daily newspaper (Columbus, Ohio), July 2, 1862.
18. William H. Herndon and Jesse W. Weik, *Abraham Lincoln: The True Story of a Great Life* (New York: D. Appleton, 1892), pp. 295–97.
19. See David S. Reynolds, *Walt Whitman's America: A Cultural Biography* (New York: Alfred A. Knopf, 1995), for a discussion of Whitman and the political crisis of the 1850s; Justin Kaplan, *Walt Whitman: A Life* (New York: Simon & Schuster, 1980), p. 215. "The Eighteenth Presidency" was finally published in 1928 in both the United States and France. See the complete text in Clifton J. Furness, *Walt Whitman's Workshop* (Cambridge: Harvard University Press, 1928), p. 99.
20. Whitman, "Eighteenth Presidency," in Furness, *Whitman's Workshop,* p. 93.
21. *The Complete Writings of Walt Whitman,* ed. Richard Maurice Bucke, Thomas B. Harned, and Horace L. Traubel (New York: G. P. Putnam's Sons, 1902), vol. 5, pp. 243–44.
22. Ibid., vol. 4, pp. 70–72, 120.
23. Walt Whitman to Nathaniel Bloom and John F. S. Gray, March 19–20, 1863, in *Walt Whitman: The Correspondence,* vol. 1, *1842–1867,* ed. Edwin Haviland Miller (New York: New York University Press, 1961), p. 81.

CHAPTER 3: "AND THE WAR CAME."

1. Richard Hofstadter, *The Progressive Historians: Turner, Beard, Parrington* (New York: Alfred A. Knopf, 1968), pp. 349–434.

2. Vernon Louis Parrington, *Main Currents in American Thought*, vol. 2, *The Romantic Revolution, 1800–1860* (New York: Harcourt, 1927), p. 158; for comments on Parrington, see Roy P. Basler, *A Touchstone for Greatness: Essays, Addresses, and Occasional Pieces About Abraham Lincoln* (Westport, Conn.: Greenwood Press, 1973), p. 77.

3. See the rhetorical analysis of Amy R. Schlegel, "Anatomy of a Masterpiece: A Close Textual Analysis of Abraham Lincoln's Second Inaugural Address," *Communication Studies*, vol. 42, no. 2 (Summer 1991), pp. 155–71.

4. Abraham Lincoln, "Address Before the Young Men's Lyceum of Springfield, Illinois," in *CW*, vol. 1, p. 108.

5. Garry Wills, *Lincoln at Gettysburg* (New York: Simon & Schuster, 1992), p. 33.

6. Abraham Lincoln, "Address Delivered at the Dedication of the Cemetery at Gettysburg," in *CW*, vol. 7, pp. 17–23.

7. David Herbert Donald, *Lincoln* (New York: Simon & Schuster, 1995), pp. 90–92; *Abraham Lincoln: A Press Portrait*, ed. Herbert Mitgang (Athens: University of Georgia Press, 1971), p. xvi.

8. Abraham Lincoln, "Brief Autobiography," in *CW*, vol. 2, p. 459.

9. Abraham Lincoln, "Autobiography Written for John L. Scripps," in ibid., vol. 4, pp. 60–67; Donald, *Lincoln*, pp. 48–51.

10. Lincoln, "Autobiography for Scripps," in *CW*, vol. 4, p. 65.

11. Abraham Lincoln, "Speech at Chicago, Illinois, July 10, 1858," in ibid., vol. 2, p. 491.

12. Edward G. Parker, *The Golden Age of Oratory* (Boston: Whittemore, Niles, Hall, 1857), p. 5.

13. Ibid., p. 7.

14. Ibid., p. 8.

15. Ibid., p. 11.

16. Abraham Lincoln, "First Inaugural Address," in *CW*, vol. 4, p. 271.

17. Ibid.

18. William H. Seward to Abraham Lincoln, Feb. 24, 1861, in John G. Nicolay and John Hay, *Abraham Lincoln: A History*, vol. 3 (New York: Century, 1890), pp. 319–20.

19. Ibid., p. 321.

20. All of these suggestions are included in the footnotes of the text of

the First Inaugural in *CW*, vol. 4, pp. 249–71, and Nicolay and Hay, *Lincoln*, vol. 3, pp. 327–44. Nicolay and Hay include the alternative last paragraph that Lincoln decided not to use at all.

21. A helpful analysis is found in Earl W. Wiley, "Abraham Lincoln: His Emergence as the Voice of the People," in *A History and Criticism of American Public Address*, ed. William Norwood Brigance, vol. 2 (New York: McGraw Hill, 1943), pp. 859–77.

22. Charles Royster, *The Destructive War* (New York: Alfred A. Knopf, 1991), p. xi.

23. Ibid., p. 292.

24. Noah Brooks, *Washington in Lincoln's Time* (New York: Century, 1896), p. 213.

CHAPTER 4: ". . . SOMEHOW THE CAUSE OF THE WAR . . ."

1. Abraham Lincoln to Albert G. Hodges, April 4, 1864, in *CW*, vol. 7, pp. 282–83n.

2. Ibid., p. 281.

3. Aristotle, *Treatise on Rhetoric*, trans. Theodore Buckley (London: Bell and Daldy, 1872), chap. 2, p. 11. See also Charles Sears Baldwin, *Ancient Rhetoric and Poetic* (New York: Macmillan, 1924), pp. 6–36.

4. George Kennedy, *The Art of Persuasion in Greece* (Princeton: Princeton University Press, 1963), pp. 88–93.

5. William Sattler, "Conceptions of ETHOS in Ancient Rhetoric," *Speech Monographs*, vol. 14 (1957), pp. 57–58.

6. Phillips Brooks, *Lectures on Preaching* (New York: E. P. Dutton, 1877), p. 5.

7. Kenneth M. Stampp, *The Peculiar Institution: Slavery in the Ante-Bellum South* (New York: Alfred A. Knopf, 1956), pp. 14–21.

8. Gabor S. Boritt, "Lincoln and the Economics of the American Dream," in *The Historian's Lincoln: Pseudohistory, Psychohistory, and History* (Urbana: University of Illinois Press, 1996), pp. 94–95. See also Boritt, *Lincoln and the Economics of the American Dream* (Memphis, Tenn.: Memphis State University Press, 1978).

9. Woodrow Wilson, *Division and Reunion: 1829–1889* (New York: Longman & Green, 1893), p. 125.

10. I am indebted to Ernest G. Bormann, a professor of speech communication, for insights on the color of language. See Bormann, *The Force of Fantasy: Restoring the American Dream* (Carbondale: Southern Illinois University Press, 1985), pp. 215ff.

11. *Liberator*, Dec. 29, 1832, quoted in Walter M. Merrill, *Against*

Wind and Tide: A Biography of Wm. Lloyd Garrison (Cambridge: Harvard University Press, 1963), p. 204; Henry Mayer, *All on Fire: William Lloyd Garrison and the Abolition of Slavery* (New York: St. Martin's Press, 1998), p. 313.

12. Merrill, *Against Wind and Tide,* pp. 204–5; Mayer, *All on Fire,* p. 313.

13. Harriet Beecher Stowe, *Uncle Tom's Cabin, or Life Among the Lowly* (Boston: John P. Jewett, 1852; reprint, Cambridge, Mass.: Belknap, 1962), pp. 452–55.

14. This question is found in Sojourner Truth, *Narrative of Sojourner Truth, with a History of Her Labors and Correspondence Drawn from her "Book of Life"* (Battle Creek, Mich.: published for the author, 1878), p. 168.

15. Edward Wagenknecht, *Harriet Beecher Stowe: The Known and Unknown* (New York: Oxford University Press, 1965), p. 185.

16. Charles Edward Stowe and Lyman Beecher Stowe, *Harriet Beecher Stowe: The Story of Her Life* (Boston: Houghton Mifflin, 1911), pp. 202–3.

17. Harriet Beecher Stowe, "Abraham Lincoln," *Littell's Living Age* (originally in *Watchman and Reflector*), Feb. 6, 1864, pp. 282–84.

18. Abraham Lincoln, "First Inaugural Address," in *CW,* vol. 4, p. 250.

19. Abraham Lincoln to Albert G. Hodges, in ibid. vol. 7, p. 281.

20. Ibid.

21. Ibid.

22. Ibid., p. 282.

23. Donald, *Lincoln,* pp. 10, 14.

CHAPTER 5: "BOTH READ THE SAME BIBLE, . . ."

1. John M. Vanderslice, *Gettysburg: A History of the Gettysburg Battle-field Memorial Association* (Philadelphia: The Memorial Association, 1897), p. 176.

2. The two vice-presidents who acceded to office because of the death of their predecessors, John Tyler and Millard Fillmore, did not give inaugural addresses.

3. These names for God are from *Inaugural Addresses of the Presidents of the United States from George Washington 1789 to John F. Kennedy 1961* (Washington, D.C.: Government Printing Office, 1961), pp. 4 (Washington), 11 (Adams), 16 (Jefferson), 25 (Madison), 45 (Monroe), 60 (Jackson), 117 (Buchanan).

4. Ibid., p. 53.

5. Henry Otis Dwight, *The Centennial History of the American Bible Society* (New York: Macmillan, 1916), pp. 271–72.

6. Charles I. Foster coined the term "Evangelical United Front" in his book *An Errand of Mercy: The Evangelical United Front, 1790–1837* (Chapel Hill: University of North Carolina Press, 1960), p. 123.

7. Orestes A. Brownson, "Abolition Proceedings," *Brownson Quarterly Review,* vol. 1 (Oct. 1838), p. 500, quoted in Arthur M. Schlesinger Jr., *Orestes A. Brownson: A Pilgrim's Progress* (Boston: Little, Brown, 1939), p. 80.

8. I am indebted to Mark Noll's thoughtful essay, "The Bible and Slavery," in *Religion and the American Civil War,* ed. Randall M. Miller, Harry S. Stout, and Charles Reagan Wilson (New York: Oxford University Press, 1998), pp. 43–73.

9. Dwight, *Centennial History,* pp. 271–72.

10. Ibid., p. 274.

11. Paul C. Gutjahr, *An American Bible: A History of the Good Book in the United States, 1777–1880* (Stanford, Calif.: Stanford University Press, 1999), pp. 126–27.

12. James M. McPherson, *For Cause and Comrades: Why Men Fought in the Civil War* (New York: Oxford University Press, 1997), pp. 62–71; John D. Pugh, pocket Bible, archives, American Bible Society.

13. Alfred Kazin, *God and the American Writer* (New York: Alfred A. Knopf, 1997), p. 132.

14. Adolphus W. Mangrum, *Myrtle Leaves, or Tokens at the Tomb* (Raleigh, N.C.: Branson & Farrar, 1864), pp. 31–32. Mangrum does not identify the name of the soldier.

15. W. Harrison Daniel, "Bible Publication and Procurement in the Confederacy," *Journal of Southern History,* vol. 24 (1958), pp. 194–97.

16. Ibid., pp. 198–99.

17. W. Edwin Hemphill, "Bibles Through the Blockade," *Commonwealth,* vol. 16 (Aug. 1949), pp. 9–12, 30–32.

18. Mentor Graham to William H. Herndon, July 15, 1865, in *Herndon's Informants: Letters, Interviews, and Statements About Abraham Lincoln,* eds. Douglas L. Wilson and Rodney O. Davis (Urbana: University of Illinois Press, 1998), pp. 75–76.

19. Joshua F. Speed to William H. Herndon, Sept. 17, 1866, in ibid., p. 342.

20. Abraham Lincoln to Mrs. Lucy G. Speed, Oct. 3, 1861, in *CW,* vol. 4, p. 546.

21. Noah Brooks, "Recollections of Abraham Lincoln," *Harper's Magazine,* vol. 30 (1865), p. 229.

22. Julia Taft Bayne, *Tad Lincoln's Father* (Boston: Little, Brown, 1931), pp. 32–33.

23. Rebecca R. Pomoroy, "What His Nurse Knew," *Magazine of His-*

tory, vol. 32, no. 1 (extra no. 125, 1926), p. 47.

24. Joshua F. Speed, *Reminiscences of Abraham Lincoln and Notes of a Visit to California* (Louisville, Ky.: J. P. Morton, 1884), pp. 32–33.

25. Abraham Lincoln, "Reply to Loyal Colored People of Baltimore upon Presentation of a Bible," Sept. 7, 1864, in *CW,* vol. 7, p. 542.

26. Noll, "Bible and Slavery," pp. 48–49.

27. Abraham Lincoln, "Farewell Address at Springfield, Illinois," in *CW,* vol. 4, pp. 190–91. Written down in pencil, as the train was leaving Springfield, the text begins in Lincoln's handwriting and ends in Nicolay's. There are two other versions of Lincoln's farewell remarks, but all conclude with essentially the same sentiment about prayer.

28. Noah Brooks to James A. Reed, Dec. 31, 1872, in Reed, "The Later Life and Religious Sentiments of Abraham Lincoln," *Scribner's Monthly,* vol. 6 (July 1873), p. 340.

29. Josiah G. Holland, *The Life of Abraham Lincoln* (Springfield, Mass.: G. Bill, 1866), pp. 236–38.

30. Seventh debate with Stephen A. Douglas at Alton, Illinois, October 15, 1858, *CW,* vol. 3, p. 315.

31. Abraham Lincoln, "Story Written for Noah Brooks," in *CW,* vol. 8, pp. 154–55.

32. Ibid., p. 155n.

33. Reinhold Niebuhr, "The Religion of Abraham Lincoln," *The Christian Century,* Feb. 10, 1965, p. 172–75.

34. Ibid., p. 173.

35. Ibid.

CHAPTER 6: "THE ALMIGHTY HAS HIS OWN PURPOSES."

1. James M. McPherson, *Battle Cry of Freedom: The Civil War Era* (New York: Oxford University Press, 1988), pp. 528–33.

2. Abraham Lincoln, "Meditation on the Divine Will," in *CW,* vol. 5, p. 404n.

3. Ibid.

4. Nicolay and Hay, in their ten-volume biography of Lincoln, observe, "The meditation was not meant to be seen by men" (vol. 6, p. 342).

5. The story of the Whig Party has been traced in rich detail by Michael Holt in *The Rise and Fall of the American Whig Party: Jacksonian Politics and the Onset of the Civil War* (New York: Oxford University Press, 1999), pp. 187–88; quotation is from Richard J. Carwardine, *Evangelicals and Politics in Antebellum America* (Knoxville: University of Tennessee Press, 1997), p. 307.

6. David Herbert Donald, *Lincoln* (New York: Simon & Schuster, 1995), pp. 566–67.

7. David Rankin Barbee, "President Lincoln and Doctor Gurley," *The Abraham Lincoln Quarterly,* vol. 5 (March 1948), p. 3.

8. *Lincoln Day by Day: A Chronology, 1809–1865,* vol. 3, 1861–1865, ed. Earl Schenck Miers (Washington, D.C.: Lincoln Sesquicentennial Commission, 1960), p. 27.

9. See George Marsden, *The Evangelical Mind and the New School Presbyterian Experience: A Case Study of Thought and Theology in 19th Century America* (New Haven, Conn.: Yale University Press, 1970).

10. "On motion, Abraham Lincoln, Henry Van Huff and Thomas Lewis were appointed a committee to aid the Rev. James Smith in a suit pending in Presbytery against this church" (Minutes of the Board of Trustees, First Presbyterian Church, 1829–1866, April 26, 1853, Illinois State Historical Library).

11. James Smith, *The Christian's Defence, Containing a Fair Statement and Impartial Examination of the Leading Objections Urged by Infidels, Against the Antiquity, Genuineness, Credibility, and Inspiration of the Holy Scriptures* (Cincinnati: J. A. James, 1843), vol. 1, p. 4.

12. Ibid., p. 4; the testimony of Edwards was contained in a lecture published by James A. Reed, then pastor of the First Presbyterian Church, Springfield, "A Lecture on the Religion of Abraham Lincoln," *Scribner's Monthly.*

13. Smith, *The Christian's Defence,* p. 4.

14. Alexander T. McGill to Rev. Phineas D. Gurley, May 1, 1860, Charles Hodge Papers, Princeton Theological Seminary Archives.

15. A. A. Hodge, *Life of Charles Hodge* (New York: Scribner, 1883), p. 521. Recent scholarship has refocused Hodge as an enormously productive theologian who, far from retreating into a fortress mentality, was busy interacting with a whole variety of intellectual crosscurrents in the middle of the nineteenth century.

16. Stephen Oates, *With Malice Toward None: A Life of Abraham Lincoln* (New York: Harper & Row, 1977), p. 29; Donald, *Lincoln,* p. 15.

17. Oates, *With Malice Toward None,* pp. 70–71, 292–93.

18. Abraham Lincoln, "Handbill Replying to Charges of Infidelity," July 31, 1846, in *CW,* vol. 1, p. 382.

19. Allen C. Guelzo, "Abraham Lincoln and the Doctrine of Necessity," *Journal of the Abraham Lincoln Association,* vol. 18, no. 1 (Winter 1997), pp. 66–67.

20. Abraham Lincoln, "Eulogy on Zachary Taylor," July 25, 1850, in *CW*, vol. 2, p. 90.

21. Francis Wharton, *A Treatise on Theism and the Modern Skeptical Theories* (Philadelphia: J. B. Lippincott, 1859), pp. 147, 152. I am grateful to Daniel W. Stowell for this source.

22. Charles Hodge, *Systematic Theology*, vol. 1 (New York: Scribner, 1871), pp. 583, 616. I am grateful to Donald K. McKim for helping me think through the issue of fatalism and providence in the Reformed tradition.

23. See Daniel W. Stowell, "Stonewall Jackson and the Providence of God," *Religion and the American Civil War*, eds. Randall M. Miller, Harry S. Stout, and Charles Reagan Wilson (New York: Oxford University Press, 1998), pp. 187–207.

24. Peyton Harrison Hoge, *Moses Drury Hoge: Life and Letters* (Richmond: Presbyterian Committee of Publication, 1889), app. 1, p. 438.

25. E. Frank Edington, *A History of the New York Avenue Presbyterian Church (1803–1961)* (Washington, D.C.: n.p., 1962), pp. 57–58; Barbee, "President Lincoln and Doctor Gurley," p. 3.

26. Phineas D. Gurley, *Southern Review* (July 1868), p. 72.

27. Phineas D. Gurley, "Funeral Address on the Occasion of the Death of William Wallace Lincoln," Washington, D.C., n.p., 1862, pp. 3–4.

28. Phineas D. Gurley, "Man's Projects and God's Results," Washington, D.C., n.p., 1863, p. 7.

29. Ibid., p. 8.

30. William E. Schenck, "A Memorial Sermon on the Life, Labours, and Christian Character of Phineas D. Gurley," Washington, D.C., 1869, p. 42.

31. Richard F. Mott, ed., *Memoir and Correspondence of Eliza P. Gurney* (Philadelphia: J. B. Lippincott, 1884), p. 307–13; Abraham Lincoln to Eliza P. Gurney, Oct. 26, 1862, in *CW*, vol. 5, p. 478n.

32. Ibid., p. 478.

33. Ibid. There is debate about the date of the letter. Donald suggests the letter was written in Sept. 1862. C. Percy Powell, the editor of vol. 3, 1861–1865, of *Lincoln Day by Day* (Washington, D.C.: n.p., 1960), correlates the interview with Mrs. Gurney with the inspiration to write the "Meditation on the Divine Will," which *CW* had dated Sept. 2, 1862.

34. Eliza P. Gurney to Abraham Lincoln, Aug. 8, 1863, in *CW*, vol. 7, pp. 535–36.

35. Abraham Lincoln to Eliza P. Gurney, Sept. 4, 1864, in ibid., pp. 535–36.

36. C. Hodge, *Systematic Theology*, vol. 1, p. 368. Gurley would have heard Hodge's thinking on divine attributes in lectures. Hodge made the decision not to publish his lectures in book form until the end of his career.

37. The Westminster Confession of Faith, chap. 2, in *The Constitution of the Presbyterian Church (U.S.A.)*, pt. 1, *Book of Confessions* (Louisville, Ky.: Office of the General Assembly, 1996), p. 128.

CHAPTER 7: ". . . EVERY DROP OF BLOOD . . ."

1. Sacvan Bercovitch, *The American Jeremiad* (Madison: University of Wisconsin Press, 1978), is the classic treatment of the jeremiad.

2. David L. Minter, *The Interpreted Design as a Structural Principle in American Prose* (New Haven: Yale University Press, 1969), pp. 50–57. Minter quotes from William Stoughton, *New Englands True Interests* (Boston: printed and sold by Nathaniel Coverly, 1774), pp. 19–20.

3. Thomas Shepherd, *A Treatise of Liturgies* (London: n.p., 1653), p. 8, quoted in Minter, *Interpreted Design*, p. 57.

4. There is debate about the authorship of the fast-day proclamations. Both Lincoln and Seward affixed their names to the proclamations, and both probably had a hand in their composition.

5. For the insights about prose-poetry I am indebted to Herbert Joseph Edwards and John Erskine Hankins, "Lincoln the Writer: The Development of His Literary Style," in *Studies in English and American Literature* (Orono: University of Maine Press, 1962), pp. 92–95.

6. In the first draft he penned *"four thousand years ago."* In the final draft he inserted *"three thousand years ago."*

7. Abraham Lincoln, "Annual Message to Congress," Dec. 1, 1862, in *CW,* vol. 5, p. 537.

8. For biographical material on Douglass, see Philip S. Foner, *Frederick Douglass: A Biography* (New York: Citadel Press, 1964); Waldo E. Martin Jr., *The Mind of Frederick Douglass* (Chapel Hill: University of North Carolina Press, 1984); and William S. McFeeley, *Frederick Douglass* (New York: W. W. Norton, 1991).

9. Christopher N. Breiseth, "Lincoln and Frederick Douglass: Another Debate," *The Journal of the Illinois State Historical Society,* vol. 68, no. 1 (Feb. 1975), pp. 11–12.

10. "'Emancipation, Racism, and the Work Before Us': An Address Delivered in Philadelphia, Pennsylvania, on 4 December 1863," in *The*

Frederick Douglass Papers, eds. John W. Blassingame and John R. McKivigan, ser. 1, vol. 3, 1855–1863 (New Haven: Yale University Press, 1991), pp. 606–7.

11. Frederick Douglass, *Autobiographies* (New York: Library of America, 1994; reprint of 1893 ed.), p. 787.

12. " 'Our Martyred President': An Address Delivered in Rochester, New York on 15 April, 1865," in Blassingame and McKivigan, *The Frederick Douglass Papers,* ser. 1, vol. 4, 1864–1880, pp. 74–79.

CHAPTER 8: "WITH MALICE TOWARD NONE; . . ."

1. Abraham Lincoln, "Address Delivered at the Cemetery at Gettysburg," in *CW,* vol. 7, p. 23.

2. Ibid.

3. In a collection of Phineas Gurley sermons at the Presbyterian Historical Society, one hears a consistent indicative-imperative refrain. Gurley first speaks about the indicative of the love of Christ, manifest in Christ's death on the cross. Gurley then calls for a selfless love as the response to Christ's love. Because these sermons are undated, they cannot be connected with Lincoln and the 1860s. Nevertheless, this was a consistent theme in Gurley's sermons.

4. Abraham Lincoln to Cuthbert Bullitt, July 28, 1862, in *CW,* vol. 5, pp. 344–46.

5. Abraham Lincoln, "Fragment on Pro-Slavery Theology," October 1, 1858[?], in ibid., vol. 3, p. 204.

6. Abraham Lincoln, "Address at Cooper Institute," Feb. 27, 1860, in ibid., p. 550.

7. Abraham Lincoln, "Address at Sanitary Fair, Baltimore, Maryland," April 18, 1864, in ibid., vol. 7, pp. 301–3.

8. The story of Fort Pillow, and what did and did not happen, is best captured in two articles: Albert Castel, "The Fort Pillow Massacre: A Fresh Examination of the Evidence," *Civil War History,* vol. 4 (1959), pp. 37–50; and John Cimprich and Robert C. Mainfort Jr., "Fort Pillow Revisited: New Evidence About an Old Controversy," *Civil War History,* vol. 28 (1982), pp. 293–306.

9. For biographical material on Forrest, see Robert Selph Henry, *"First with the Most" Forrest* (Indianapolis: Bobbs-Merrill, 1944); and Jack Hurst, *Nathan Bedford Forrest: A Biography* (New York: Alfred A. Knopf, 1993). Sherman's assessment is in U.S. War Department, *The War of Rebellion: A Compilation of the Official Records*

of the Union and Confederate Armies (Washington, D.C.: n.p., 1889), ser. no. 78, pp. 121, 142.

10. Cimprich and Mainfort Jr., "Fort Pillow Revisited," p. 297.

11. Abraham Lincoln, "To Cabinet Members," May 3, 1864, in *CW,* vol. 7, pp. 328–29; a summary of the Cabinet responses is found in Nicolay and Hay, *Abraham Lincoln: A History,* vol. 6, pp. 478ff.

12. Roy Basler, "And for His Widow and His Orphan," *Quarterly Journal of the Library of Congress,* vol. 27, no. 4 (Oct. 1970), pp. 290–94.

13. Abraham Lincoln to Charles Sumner, May 19, 1864, in *CW,* suppl., p. 243.

14. *Chicago Tribune,* March 22, 1865, p. 2.

CHAPTER 9: ". . . BETTER THAN ANYTHING . . ."

1. *New York World,* March 6, 1865, p. 3.
2. *New York Herald,* March 6, 1865, p. 5.
3. Ibid.
4. Ibid.
5. A. B. Bradford to Simon Cameron, March 8, 1865, Simon Cameron Papers, Library of Congress.
6. Frederick Douglass, *Autobiographies* (New York: Library of America, 1994; reprint of 1893 ed.), p. 801.
7. Ibid., p. 802.
8. Charles Francis Adams Jr. to his father, March 7, 1865, in *A Cycle of Adams Letters, 1861–1865,* ed. Worthington Chauncey Ford, vol. 2 (New York: Houghton Mifflin, 1920), p. 257.
9. Abraham Lincoln to Mrs. Amanda H. Hall, March 20, 1865, in *CW,* vol. 8, p. 367; see also Ronald H. Carpenter, "In Not-So-Trivial Pursuit of Rhetorical Wedgies: An Historical Approach to Lincoln's Second Inaugural Address," in *Communication Reports,* Winter 1988, p. 79.
10. Abraham Lincoln to Mrs. Amanda H. Hall, March 20, 1865, in *CW,* vol. 8, p. 367n. There is no doubt that the facsimiles were made from the original letter. At the time of *The Collected Works of Abraham Lincoln* (1953–55), the editors were not able to certify the location or ownership of the original letter. The original was subsequently acquired by the Illinois State Historical Society in the 1970s.
11. *Abraham Lincoln: A Press Portrait,* ed. Herbert Mitgang (Athens: University of Georgia Press, 1971), p. xviii. Mitgang surveys newspapers, always attempting to present both sides, in twenty states

and the District of Columbia. He includes publications supporting both the Union and the Confederacy.

12. Ibid., pp. xvii–xviii; Robert S. Harper, *Lincoln and the Press* (New York: McGraw Hill, 1951), p. 223.

13. Abraham Lincoln, "Second Lecture on Discoveries and Inventions," Feb. 11, 1859, in *CW,* vol. 3, p. 362.

14. Harper, *Lincoln and the Press,* p. 289. John W. Forney, publisher of Washington's *Daily Morning Chronicle,* described Marble and the *World:* "The most malignant, the most brutal, the most false and scurrilous of all the assailants of the President and the Republican Party during the past year or two, has been the New York World."

15. Quoted in Harper, *Lincoln and the Press,* p. 97.

16. *New York Times,* March 6, 1865.

17. *New York Herald,* March 5, 1865, p. 4.

18. Ibid.

19. *New York World,* March 6, 1865.

20. *Chicago Times,* March 6, 1865, p. 2.

21. *Daily Illinois State Register,* March 8, 1865.

22. *Philadelphia Inquirer,* March 6, 1865.

23. *Washington (D.C.) Daily National Intelligencer,* March 6, 1865.

24. *Jersey City Times,* March 6, 1865, p. 2.

25. *Richmond Examiner,* n.d., quoted in *Chicago Tribune,* March 10, 1865, p. 1.

26. *Petersburg (Va.) Daily Express,* March 9, 1865.

27. *Daily National Intelligencer,* March 6, 1865, p. 2.

28. *New York World,* March 6, 1865.

29. *Times* (London), March 17, 1865, p. 9.

30. *Spectator* (London), March 25, 1865, quoted in *Chicago Tribune,* April 18, 1865, p. 2.

31. *Saturday Review,* March 18, 1865, quoted in ibid., p. 87.

32. John Bigelow, *Retrospections of an Active Life* (New York: Baker & Taylor, 1909–13), vol. 2, p. 429. I am indebted to Charles Royster for this source.

33. *Chicago Tribune,* April 12, 1865, p. 2, based on report from Paris, March 21, 1865.

34. Abraham Lincoln to Thurlow Weed, March 15, 1865, in *CW,* vol. 8, p. 356. No letter from Weed mentioning this material has been found.

35. Ibid.; Abraham Lincoln, "Meditation on the Divine Will," in ibid., vol. 5, p. 404; Abraham Lincoln to Eliza Gurney, October 26, 1862, in ibid., vol. 5, p. 478.

36. Maggie Lindsley, *Maggie Lindsley's Journal* (n.p.: privately printed,

1977), p. 73; *Through Five Administrations: Reminiscences of Colonel William H. Crook,* compiled and edited by Margarita Spalding Gerry (New York: Harper, 1907), p. 26.

37. Douglass, *Life and Times,* p. 402. Douglass believed that the rebuff at the door was not at anyone's direction, but simply continued the usual custom of treatment toward African Americans.

EPILOGUE

1. I have read with appreciation Garry Wills's "Lincoln's Greatest Speech?" in *The Atlantic Monthly,* September 1, 1999, p. 60–70. William Lee Miller's essay, "Lincoln's Second Inaugural: The Zenith of Statecraft," in *The Center Magazine,* July/August 1980, pp. 53–64, was a valuable resource at the beginning of my explorations.
2. Abraham Lincoln to Thurlow Weed, March 15, 1865, in *CW,* vol. 8, p. 356.

APPENDIX II

1. Abraham Lincoln to Albert G. Hodges, April 4, 1864, in *CW,* vol. 7, pp. 282–83.

APPENDIX III

1. Abraham Lincoln, "Meditation on the Divine Will," Lincoln Collection, John Hay Library, Brown University.

BIBLIOGRAPHY

In the midst of the continuing debates about reminiscence—he said, she said, often years after Lincoln—one is on solid ground in returning again and again to Lincoln's own words. The Lincoln papers are published in Roy P. Basler, ed., *The Collected Works of Abraham Lincoln,* 9 vols. (New Brunswick, N.J.: 1953–55) and in *The Collected Works of Abraham Lincoln, Supplement,* 1832–1865 (New Brunswick, N.J.: 1974). For a comprehensive evaluation of remarks attributed to Lincoln, see Don E. Fehrenbacher and Virginia Fehrenbacher, eds., *Recollected Words of Abraham Lincoln* (Stanford, Calif.: Stanford University Press, 1996).

The best introduction to the whole Civil War era is James M. McPherson's highly readable *Battle Cry of Freedom: The Civil War Era* (New York: Oxford University Press, 1988), which won the Pulitzer Prize in 1990. A fine complementary volume is *Religion and the Civil War,* edited by Randall M. Miller, Harry S. Stout, and Charles Reagan Wilson (New York: Oxford University Press, 1998).

Biographies of Lincoln began before he was dead. The best of the past three generations are Benjamin Thomas, *Abraham Lincoln: A Biography* (New York: Alfred A. Knopf, 1952); Stephen B. Oates, *With Malice Toward None: The Life of Abraham Lincoln* (New York: Harper & Row, 1977); and David Herbert Donald, *Lincoln* (New York: Simon & Schuster, 1995). Allen C. Guelzo's *Abraham Lincoln: Redeemer President* (Grand Rapids, Mich.: W. B. Eerdmans, 1999) focuses on Lincoln as a man of intellectual curiosity and ideas.

Rhetoric, so central in Lincoln's day in both academic and popular culture, is the matrix in which to understand the Second Inaugural as an address. A classic treatment of the tension between so-called refined and vulgar speech is Kenneth Cmiel's *Democratic Eloquence: The Fight over Popular Speech in Nineteenth-Century America* (Berkeley: University of California, 1990). Nan Johnson offers a fine overview of *Nineteenth-Century Rhetoric in North America* (Carbondale: Southern Illinois University Press, 1991).

The following is a selected bibliography.

BOOKS

Aristotle. *Treatise on Rhetoric*. Theodore Buckley, trans. London: Bell and Daldy, 1872.

Allen, William C. *The Dome of the United States Capitol: An Architectural History*. Washington, D.C.: Government Printing Office, 1992.

Baldwin, Charles Sears. *Ancient Rhetoric and Poetic*. New York: Macmillan, 1924.

Barondess, Benjamin. *Three Lincoln Masterpieces*. Charleston: Education Foundation of West Virginia, Inc., 1954.

Basler, Roy P. *A Touchstone for Greatness: Essays, Addresses, and Occasional Pieces about Abraham Lincoln*. Westport, Conn.: Greenwood Press, 1973.

———, ed. *The Collected Works of Abraham Lincoln*, 9 vols. New Brunswick, N.J.: 1953–55; and supplement, 1832–1865 [1974].

Bayne, Julia Taft. *Tad Lincoln's Father*. Boston: Little, Brown, 1931.

Bennett, Lerone, Jr. *Forced into Glory: Abraham Lincoln's White Dream*. Chicago: Johnson Publishing Company, 2000.

Benson, Thomas W., ed. *Rhetorical and Political Culture in Nineteenth-Century America*. East Lansing: Michigan State University Press, 1997.

Bercovitch, Sacvan. *The American Jeremiad*. Madison: University of Wisconsin Press, 1978.

Black, Edwin. *Rhetorical Criticism: A Study in Method*. Madison: University of Wisconsin Press, 1978.

Blight, David W. *Frederick Douglass' Civil War: Keeping Faith in Jubilee*. Baton Rouge: Louisiana State University Press, 1989.

Bigelow, John. *Retrospections of an Active Life*. New York: Baker & Taylor, 1909–1913.

Bloom, Harold. *Poetry and Repression*. New Haven, Conn.: Yale University Press, 1976.

Boritt, Gabor S. *Lincoln and the Economics of the American Dream*. Memphis, Tenn.: Memphis State University Press, 1978.

———, ed. *The Historian's Lincoln: Pseudohistory, Psychohistory, and History*. Urbana: University of Illinois Press, 1996.

Bormann, Ernest G. *The Force of Fantasy: Restoring the American Dream*.

Carbondale: Southern Illinois University Press, 1985.

Braden, Waldo W. *Abraham Lincoln: Public Speaker*. Baton Rouge: Louisiana State University Press, 1988.

Brooks, Noah. *Washington in Lincoln's Time*. New York: Century, 1896.

Brown, Francis. *Raymond of the Times*. New York: W. W. Norton, 1951.

Burlingame, Michael. *The Inner World of Abraham Lincoln*. Urbana: University of Illinois Press, 1994.

————, ed. *Lincoln Observed: Civil War Dispatches of Noah Brooks*. Baltimore: Johns Hopkins University Press, 1998.

————, ed. *An Oral History of Abraham Lincoln: John G. Nicolay's Interviews and Essays*. Carbondale: Southern Illinois University Press, 1996.

Carpenter, Francis B. *The Inner Life of Abraham Lincoln: Six Months at the White House*. New York: Hurd and Houghton, 1874.

Carwardine, Richard J. *Evangelicals and Politics in Antebellum America*. Knoxville: University of Tennessee, 1997.

Charnwood, Godfrey Rathdorp Benson. *Life of Abraham Lincoln*. New York: Henry Holt, 1916.

Cmiel, Kenneth. *Democratic Eloquence: The Fight over Popular Speech in Nineteenth-Century America*. Berkeley: University of California Press, 1990.

Cornish, Dudley Taylor. *The Sable Arm: Black Troops in the Union Army, 1861–1865*. Lawrence: University Press of Kansas, 1956.

Cox, LaWanda. *Lincoln and Black Freedom: A Study in Presidential Leadership*. Urbana: University of Illinois Press, 1985.

Cox, LaWanda, and John H. Cox. *Politics, Principle, and Prejudice, 1865–1866*. Glencoe, N.Y.: Free Press, 1963.

Davis, Cullam, Charles B. Strozier, Rebecca Monroe Veach, and Geoffrey C. Ward, eds. *The Public and Private Lincoln: Contemporary Perspectives*. Carbondale: Southern Illinois University Press, 1979.

Dickens, Charles. *American Notes*. London: Chapman and Hall, 1842.

Diggins, John Patrick. *The Lost Soul of American Politics: Virtue, Self-Interest, and the Foundations of Liberalism*. New York: Basic Books, 1984.

————. *On Hallowed Ground: Abraham Lincoln and the Foundations of American History*. New Haven, Conn.: Yale University Press, 2000.

Donald, David Herbert. *Lincoln*. New York: Simon & Schuster, 1995.

Dwight, Henry Otis. *The Centennial History of the American Bible Society*. New York: Macmillan, 1916.

Fehrenbacher, Don E. *Lincoln in Text and Context*. Stanford, Calif.: Stanford University Press, 1984.

Fehrenbacher, Don E., Virginia Fehrenbacher, and Mark E. Neely Jr., eds.

Recollected Words of Abraham Lincoln. Stanford, Calif.: Stanford University Press, 1996.

Fischer, Roger A. *Tippecanoe and Trinkets Too: The Material Culture of American Presidential Campaigns, 1828–1984*. Urbana: University of Illinois Press, 1988.

Foner, Philip S. *Frederick Douglass: A Biography*. New York: Citadel Press, 1964.

Ford, Worthington Chauncey, ed. *A Cycle of Adams Letters, 1861–1865*. New York: Houghton Mifflin, 1920.

Foster, Charles I. *An Errand of Mercy: The Evangelical United Front, 1790–1837*. Chapel Hill: University of North Carolina Press, 1960.

French, Benjamin Brown. *Witness to the Young Republic: A Yankee's Journal, 1828–1870*. Hanover, N.H.: University Press of New England, 1989.

Furness, Clifton J. *Walt Whitman's Workshop*. Cambridge: Harvard University Press, 1928.

Gerry, Margarita Spalding, ed. *Through Five Administrations: Reminiscences of Colonel William H. Crook*. New York: Harper and Brothers, 1907.

Greenstone, J. David. *The Lincoln Persuasion: Remaking American Liberalism*. Princeton, N.J.: Princeton University Press, 1993.

Guelzo, Allen C. *Abraham Lincoln: Redeemer President*. Grand Rapids, Mich.: W. B. Eerdmans, 1999.

Gurley, Phineas D. *Faith in God: Dr. Gurley's Sermon at the Funeral of Abraham Lincoln*. From the Original Manuscript. Philadelphia: Department of History of the Office of the General Assembly of the Presbyterian Church in the U.S.A., 1940.

Gutjahr, Paul C. *An American Bible: A History of the Good Book in the United States, 1777–1880*. Stanford, Calif.: Stanford University Press, 1999.

Harper, Robert S. *Lincoln and the Press*. New York: McGraw Hill, 1951.

Harris, William C. *With Charity for All: Lincoln and the Restoration of the Union*. Lexington: University Press of Kentucky, 1997.

Herndon, William H., and Jesse W. Weik. *Abraham Lincoln: The True Story of a Great Life*. New York: D. Appleton, 1892.

Henry, Robert Selph. *"First with the Most" Forrest*. Indianapolis: Bobbs-Merrill, 1944.

Hodge, A. A. *Life of Charles Hodge*. New York: Charles Scribner's Sons, 1883.

Hodge, Charles. *Systematic Theology*, vol. 1. New York: Charles Scribner's Sons, 1871.

Hofstadter, Richard. *The Progressive Historians: Turner, Beard, Parrington*. New York: Alfred A. Knopf, 1968.

Holt, Michael. *The Rise and Fall of the American Whig Party: Jacksonian*

Politics and the Onset of the Civil War. New York: Oxford University Press, 1999.

Holzer, Harold, Gabor S. Boritt, and Mark E. Neely Jr. *Changing the Lincoln Image.* Fort Wayne, Ind.: Louis A. Warren Lincoln Library and Museum, 1985.

———. *The Lincoln Image: Abraham Lincoln and the Popular Print.* New York: Scribner, 1984.

Howe, Daniel Walker. *The Political Culture of the American Whigs.* Chicago: University of Chicago Press, 1979.

Hurst, Jack. *Nathan Bedford Forrest: A Biography.* New York: Alfred A. Knopf, 1993.

Inaugural Addresses of the Presidents of the United States from George Washington 1789 to John F. Kennedy 1961. Washington, D.C.: Government Printing Office, 1961.

Jaffe, Harry V. *Crisis of the House Divided: An Interpretation of the Issues in the Lincoln-Douglas Debates.* Seattle: University of Washington Press, 1959.

Johnson, Nan. *Nineteenth-Century Rhetoric in North America.* Carbondale: Southern Illinois University Press, 1991.

Kaplan, Justin. *Walt Whitman: A Life.* New York: Simon & Schuster, 1980.

Kazin, Alfred. *God and the American Writer.* New York: Alfred A. Knopf, 1997.

Kennedy, George. *The Art of Persuasion in Greece.* Princeton: Princeton University Press, 1963.

Lately, Thomas. *The First President Johnson.* New York: William Morrow, 1968.

Leech, Margaret. *Reveille in Washington: 1860–1865.* New York: Harper & Brothers, 1941.

Lindsley, Maggie. *Maggie Lindsley's Journal.* N.p.: privately printed, 1977.

Marsden, George. *The Evangelical Mind and the New School Presbyterian Experience: A Case Study of Thought and Theology in 19th Century America.* New Haven, Conn.: Yale University Press, 1970.

Martin, Waldo E., Jr. *The Mind of Frederick Douglass.* Chapel Hill: University of North Carolina Press, 1984.

Mayer, Henry. *All on Fire: William Lloyd Garrison and the Abolition of Slavery.* New York: St. Martin's Press, 1998.

McFeeley, William S. *Frederick Douglass.* New York: W. W. Norton, 1991.

McPherson, James M. *Abraham Lincoln and the Second American Revolution.* New York: Oxford University Press, 1990.

———. *Battle Cry of Freedom: The Civil War Era.* New York: Oxford University Press, 1988.

————. *Drawn with the Sword: Reflections on the American Civil War.* New York: Oxford University Press, 1996.

————. *For Cause and Comrades: Why Men Fought in the Civil War.* New York: Oxford University Press, 1997.

McPherson, James M., ed. *"We Cannot Escape History": Lincoln and the Last Best Hope of Earth.* Urbana: University of Illinois Press, 1995.

Miller, Randall M., Harry S. Stout, and Charles Reagan Wilson, eds. *Religion and the American Civil War.* New York: Oxford University Press, 1998.

Milton, George Fort. *The Age of Hate: Andrew Johnson and the Radicals.* New York: Coward-McCann, 1930.

Minter, David L. *The Interpreted Design as a Structural Principle in American Prose.* New Haven, Conn.: Yale University Press, 1969.

Mitgang, Herbert, ed. *Abraham Lincoln: A Press Portrait.* Athens: University of Georgia Press, 1971.

Moorhead, James H. *American Apocalypse: Yankee Protestants and the Civil War, 1860–1869.* New Haven, Conn.: Yale University Press, 1948.

Morgenthau, Hans J., and David Hein. *Essays on Lincoln's Faith and Politics,* vol. 6. Kenneth W. Thompson, ed. Lanham, Md.: University Press of America, 1983.

Morel, Lucas E. *Lincoln's Sacred Effort: Defining Religion's Role in American Self-Government.* Lanham, Md.: Lexington Books, 2000.

Mott, Richard F., ed. *Memoir and Correspondence of Eliza P. Gurney.* Philadelphia: J. B. Lippincott, 1884.

Newman, Ralph G., ed. *Lincoln for the Ages.* Garden City, N.Y.: Doubleday, 1966.

Nicolay, John G., and John Hay. *Abraham Lincoln: A History,* vol. 3. New York: Century, 1890.

Noll, Mark, ed. *The Princeton Theology, 1812–1921.* Grand Rapids, Mich.: Baker, 1983.

Oates, Stephen. *With Malice Toward None: A Life of Abraham Lincoln.* New York: Harper & Row, 1977.

Paludan, Philip Shaw. *"A People's Contest": The Union and the Civil War, 1861–1865.* New York: Harper & Row, 1988.

Parker, Edward G. *The Golden Age of Oratory.* Boston: Whittemore, Niles, Hall, 1857.

Parrington, Vernon Louis. *Main Currents in American Thought, vol. 2, The Romantic Revolution, 1800–1860.* New York: Harcourt, 1927.

Peterson, Merrill D. *Lincoln in American Memory.* New York: Oxford University Press, 1994.

Powell, C. Percy, ed. *Lincoln Day by Day. Volume 3: 1861–1865.* Washington, D.C.: n.p., 1960.

Randall, J. G., and Richard N. Current. *Lincoln the President: Last Full*

Measure. New York: Dodd, Mead & Company, 1955.

Reynolds, David S. *Walt Whitman's America: A Cultural Biography*. New York: Alfred A. Knopf, 1995.

Rose, Anne C. *Victorian America and the Civil War*. Cambridge: Cambridge University Press, 1992.

Royster, Charles. *The Destructive War*. New York: Alfred A. Knopf, 1991.

Schlesinger, Arthur M., Jr. *Orestes A. Brownson: A Pilgrim's Progress*. Boston: Little, Brown, 1939.

Shepherd, Thomas. *A Treatise of Liturgies*. London: n.p., 1653.

Smith, James. *The Christian's Defence, Containing a Fair Statement and Impartial Examination of the Leading Objections Urged by Infidels, Against the Antiquity, Genuineness, Credibility and Inspiration of the Holy Scriptures*. Cincinnati: J. A. James, 1843.

Smith, William R. *The Rhetoric of American Politics: A Study of Documents*. Westport, Conn.: Greenwood Press, 1969.

Stampp, Kenneth M. *The Peculiar Institution: Slavery in the Ante-Bellum South*. New York: Alfred A. Knopf, 1956.

Stowe, Charles Edward, and Lyman Beecher Stowe. *Harriet Beecher Stowe: The Story of Her Life*. Boston: Houghton Mifflin, 1911.

Stowe, Harriet Beecher. *Uncle Tom's Cabin, or Life Among the Lowly*. Boston: John P. Jewett, 1852; reprint, Cambridge, Mass.: Belknap Press, 1962.

Sweet, Timothy. *Traces of War: Poetry, Photography, and the Crisis of Union*. Baltimore: Johns Hopkins University Press, 1990.

Thomas, Benjamin. *Abraham Lincoln: A Biography*. New York: Alfred A. Knopf, 1952.

Thurow, Glen E. *Abraham Lincoln and American Political Religion*. Albany: State University of New York Press, 1976.

Tompkins, Jane P. *Reader-Response Criticism: From Formalism to Post-Structuralism*. Baltimore: Johns Hopkins University Press, 1980.

Trefousse, Hans L. *Andrew Johnson: A Biography*. New York: W.W. Norton, 1989.

Vanderslice, John M. *Gettysburg: A History of the Gettysburg Battle-field Memorial Association*. Philadelphia: The Memorial Association, 1897.

Vorenberg, Michael. *Final Freedom: The Civil War, the Abolition of Slavery, and the Thirteenth Amendment*. Cambridge: Cambridge University Press, 2001.

Wagenknecht, Edward. *Harriet Beecher Stowe: The Known and Unknown*. New York: Oxford University Press, 1965.

Wharton, Francis. *A Treatise on Theism and the Modern Skeptical Theories*. Philadelphia: J. B. Lippincott, 1859.

White, James Boyd. *When Words Lose Their Meaning: Constitutions and*

Reconstitutions of Language, Character, and Community. Chicago: University of Chicago Press, 1984.

Wills, Garry. *Lincoln at Gettysburg.* New York: Simon & Schuster, 1992.

Wilson, Douglas L. *Honor's Voice: The Transformation of Abraham Lincoln.* New York: Alfred A. Knopf, 1998.

Wilson, Douglas L., and Rodney O. Davis, eds. *Herndon's Informants: Letters, Interviews, and Statements About Abraham Lincoln.* Urbana: University of Illinois Press, 1998.

Wilson, Edmund. *Patriotic Gore: Studies in the Literature of the American Civil War.* New York: Oxford University Press, 1962.

Wilson, Woodrow. *Division and Reunion: 1829–1889.* New York: Longman and Green, 1893.

Wolf, William J. *The Almost Chosen People: A Study of the Religion of Abraham Lincoln.* Garden City, N.Y.: Doubleday, 1959.

CHAPTERS IN BOOKS AND JOURNAL ARTICLES

Angle, Paul M. "Lincoln's Power with Words." *Abraham Lincoln Association Papers* (1935): 59–87.

Aune, James Arnt. "Lincoln and the American Sublime." *Communication Reports* (Winter 1988): 70–75.

Barbee, David Rankin. "President Lincoln and Doctor Gurley." *The Abraham Lincoln Quarterly* 5 (March 1948): 3.

Barzun, Jacques. "Lincoln the Writer," in *Jacques Barzun on Writing, Editing and Publishing,* 2nd ed. Chicago: University of Chicago Press, 1972, pp. 65–81.

Basler, Roy P. "And for His Widow and His Orphan." *Quarterly Journal of the Library of Congress* 27, no. 4 (October 1970): 290–94.

Berry, Mildred Freburg. "Abraham Lincoln: His Development in the Skills of the Platform," in *A History and Criticism of American Public Address,* vol. 2, William Norwood Brigance, ed. New York: McGraw-Hill, 1943, pp. 828–57.

Boritt, Gabor S. "Lincoln and the Economics of the American Dream," in *The Historian's Lincoln: Pseudohistory, Psychohistory, and History,* Gabor S. Boritt, ed. Urbana: University of Illinois Press, 1996.

Brauer, Gerald C. "An Almost Sacred Text: Lincoln's Second Inaugural Address." The Hewlett Lecture, Graduate Theological Union, Berkeley, Calif., February 9, 1999. Paper given to author.

Breiseth, Christopher N. "Lincoln and Frederick Douglass: Another Debate." *Journal of the Illinois State Historical Society* 68, no. 1 (February 1975): 11–12.

Brooks, Noah. "Personal Reminiscences of Lincoln." *Scribner's Monthly* 15 (February 1878): 561–69.

———. "Personal Reminiscences of Lincoln." *Scribner's Monthly* 15 (March 1878): 673–81.

———. "Recollections of Abraham Lincoln." *Harper's Magazine* 30 (1865): 229.

——— (to James A. Reed). "The Later Life and Religious Sentiments of Abraham Lincoln." *Scribner's Monthly* 6 (July 1873): 340.

Carpenter, Ronald H. "In Not-So-Trivial Pursuit of Rhetorical Wedgies: An Historical Approach to Lincoln's Second Inaugural Address." *Communication Reports* (Winter 1988): 79.

Carwardine, Richard J. "Lincoln: Evangelical Religion and American Political Culture in the Era of the Civil War." *Journal of the Abraham Lincoln Association* 18, no. 1 (Winter 1997): 27–55.

Castel, Albert. "The Fort Pillow Massacre: A Fresh Examination of the Evidence." *Civil War History* 4 (1959): 37–50.

Cimprich, John, and Robert C. Mainfort Jr. "Fort Pillow Revisited: New Evidence About an Old Controversy." *Civil War History* 28 (1982): 293–306.

Daniel, W. Harrison. "Bible Publication and Procurement in the Confederacy." *Journal of Southern History* 24 (1958): 194–97.

Delbanco, Andrew. "Lincoln and Modernity," in *Knowledge and Belief in America: Enlightenment Traditions and Modern Religious Thought,* William M. Shea and Peter A. Huff, eds. Cambridge: Cambridge University Press, 1995, pp. 247–69.

Edwards, Herbert Joseph, and John Erskine Hankins. "Lincoln the Writer: The Development of His Literary Style." *Studies in English and American Literature.* Orono: University of Maine Press, 1962.

Frederickson, George M. "The Search for Order and Community," in *The Public and the Private Lincoln: Contemporary Perspectives.* Carbondale: Southern Illinois University Press, 1949, pp. 86–98.

Grossman, Allen. "The Poetics of Union in Whitman and Lincoln: An Inquiry Toward the Relationship of Art and Policy," in *The American Renaissance Reconsidered,* Walter Ben Michaels and Donald E. Pease, eds. Baltimore: Johns Hopkins University Press, 1985.

Guelzo, Allen C. "Abraham Lincoln and the Doctrine of Necessity." *Journal of the Abraham Lincoln Association* 18, no. 1 (Winter 1997): 57–81.

Hein, David. "Research on Lincoln's Religious Beliefs and Practices: A Bibliographical Essay." *Lincoln Herald* 86, no. 1 (Spring 1984): 2–5.

Howe, Daniel Walker. "The Evangelical Movement and Political Culture in the North During the Second Party System." *The Journal of American History* 77, no. 4 (March 1991): 1216–39.

Hurt, James. "All the Living and the Dead: Lincoln's Imagery." *American Literature* 52 (1980): 351–80.

Leff, Michael. "Dimensions of Temporality in Lincoln's Second Inaugural," in *Readings in Rhetorical Criticism*, Carl R. Burgchardt, ed. State College, Penn.: Strata Publications, 1995.

Miller, William Lee. "Lincoln's Second Inaugural: The Zenith of Statecraft." *The Center Magazine* 13, no. 4 (July/August 1980): 53–64.

Nevins, Allan. "Lincoln in His Writings," introduction to *The Life and Writings of Abraham Lincoln*, Philip Van Doren Stern, ed. New York: Random House, 1940, pp. xvii–xxvii.

Nichols, Marie Hochmuth. "Lincoln's First Inaugural," in *Methods of Rhetorical Criticism: A Twentieth-Century Perspective*, Robert L. Scott and Bernard L. Brock, eds. New York: Harper & Row, 1972.

Niebuhr, Reinhold. "The Religion of Abraham Lincoln." *The Christian Century* (February 10, 1965): 172–75.

Noll, Mark. "The Bible and Slavery," in *Religion and the American Civil War*, Randall M. Miller, Harry S. Stout, and Charles Regan Wilson, eds. New York: Oxford University Press, 1998.

———. "Both . . . Pray to the Same God: The Singularity of Lincoln's Faith in the Era of the Civil War." *Journal of the Abraham Lincoln Association* 18, no. 1 (Winter 1997): 1–26.

———. "The Struggle for Lincoln's Soul." *Books and Culture: A Christian Review* (September/October 1995): 3–7.

Parrillo, Nicholas. "Lincoln's Calvinist Transformation: Emancipation and War." *Civil War History* 46, no. 3 (2000): 227–53.

Pomoroy, Rebecca R. "What His Nurse Knew." *The Magazine of History* 32, no. 1, extra no. 125 (1926): 47.

Schenck, William E. "A Memorial Sermon on the Life, Labours, and Christian Character of Phineas D. Gurley." Washington, D.C., 1869.

Schlegel, Amy R. "Anatomy of a Masterpiece: A Close Textual Analysis of Abraham Lincoln's Second Inaugural Address." *Communication Studies* 42, no. 2 (Summer 1991): 155–71.

Silbey, Joel. "'Always a Whig in Politics': The Partisan Life of Abraham Lincoln." *Papers of the Abraham Lincoln Association* 7 (1985): 21–42.

Solomon, Martha. "'With Firmness in the Right': The Creation of Moral Hegemony in Lincoln's Second Inaugural." *Communication Reports* (Winter 1988).

Stowe, Harriet Beecher. "Abraham Lincoln." *Littell's Living Age* (originally in *Watchman and Reflector*) (February 6, 1864): 282–84.

Stowell, Daniel W. "Stonewall Jackson and the Providence of God," in *Re-*

ligion and the American Civil War, Randall M. Miller, Harry S. Stout, and Charles Regan Wilson, eds. New York: Oxford University Press, 1998.

Wichelns, Herbert A. "The Literary Criticism of Oratory," in *Studies in Rhetoric and Public Speaking in Honor of James Albert Winans, by Pupils and Colleagues.* New York: The Century Company, 1925.

Wiley, Earl W. "Abraham Lincoln: His Emergence as the Voice of the People," in *A History and Criticism of American Public Address,* William Norwood Brigance II, ed. New York: McGraw-Hill, 1943, pp. 859–77.

Zarefsky, David. "Approaching Lincoln's Second Inaugural Address," in *The Practice of Rhetorical Criticism,* 2nd ed. James R. Andrews, ed. New York: Longman, 1990.

PH.D. DISSERTATIONS

Chantrill, Patricia A. *Reclaiming the Fugitive in Lincoln's First Inaugural Address.* Ph.D. dissertation, Washington State University, 1997.

Morel, Lucas E. *The Role of Religion in Abraham Lincoln's Statesmanship: Moderating the Influence of Religion in a Self-Governing Regime While Preserving Its Legitimate Claim on the Souls of the Nation.* Ph.D. dissertation, Claremont Graduate School, 1994.

Winger, Stewart Lance. *Lincoln's Religious Rhetoric: American Romanticism and the Anti-Slavery Impulse.* Ph.D. dissertation, University of Chicago, 1998.

NEWSPAPERS

Chicago Times
Chicago Tribune
Daily Illinois State Register
Illinois Daily State Journal
New-York Daily Tribune
New York Herald
The New York Times
New-York World
The Philadelphia Inquirer
Sacramento Daily Union
Times (London)
Washington (D.C.) Daily National Intelligencer

Index to Other Lincoln Texts

ACKNOWLEDGMENTS

Each day as I worked on the Second Inaugural I have been conscious that I was standing on the shoulders of Lincoln scholars of the past. I was humbled just as one feels when entering territory in the western United States staked out by eminent pioneers. More than any endnotes can tell, I have been the beneficiary of the work of countless researchers and writers, even when I found myself attempting to construct new trails away from well-worn paths.

I am indebted to librarians, many of whom have become friends and consultants along the way. My special gratitude is to my home base, The Huntington Library, Art Collections, and Botanical Gardens, to which I dedicate this book. The staff, and a host of "readers," have created an unparalleled ethos for research and writing. I wish to thank Robert Allen Skotheim, President; Robert C. Ritchie, W. M. Keck Director of Research; and David S. Zeidberg, Avery Director of the Library. John Rhodehamel, Norris Foundation Curator, American Historical Manuscripts, offered his continuing interest and counsel. My daily thanks are to Christopher J. S. Adde, Jill Cogan, and Susi Krasnoo of the Readers Services Department who have been attentive to every question and need. The marvelous gardens, their plants and flowers changing from fall to winter to spring, have become an oasis in which to wander and to think.

At the Library of Congress, John R. Sellers, Historical Specialist for the Civil War and Reconstruction, has become a point man suggesting people to talk with and opening doors with his telephone calls. I especially want to thank Mary Ison and her staff of the Photography and Prints Division.

At the Smithsonian National Museum of American History, Harry Rubenstein, Curator of the Political History Collections, was the recipient of one such telephone call. On short notice, on a January afternoon when a member of President George W. Bush's inaugural committee was coming to visit, he took me up into the "attic" of the museum to inspect the artifacts related to the 1864 election and Lincoln's Second Inaugural.

The Illinois State Historical Library at Springfield, Illinois, has become an unending resource of manuscripts and people. First, Thomas F. Schwartz (now Historian for the State of Illinois), and then Kim Bauer, have been my hosts. Daniel W. Stowell not only introduced me to the Lincoln Legal Project but shared his interest and knowledge in some of my questions.

I traveled to the Lincoln Collection at the John Jay Library at Brown University expressly to see the "Meditation on the Divine Will." I want to thank Mary Jo Kline who guided me through the breadth of this impressive Lincoln collection.

At the Lincoln Museum at Fort Wayne, Indiana, I was provided excerpts from newspapers that related to the Second Inaugural. Curator Don McCue offered me his help at the Lincoln Shrine at Redlands, California.

My research and writing interests have taken me to resources beyond the usual Lincoln places. At the American Bible Society I was deeply moved as I examined nearly a hundred pocket Bibles once carried by Union and Confederate soldiers. I wish to thank Mary Cordato, Mary Deptula, and Liana Lupas for their assistance.

Jonathan H. Mann, publisher of *The Rail Splitter,* opened the world of Lincoln collectors to me. Donald Ackerman made available from his private collection the stevensgraph multicolored ribbon and the ribbon including the Alexander Gardner photograph of Lincoln, both sold or distributed at the Second Inaugural.

At Princeton Theological Seminary, while on the trail of information on Charles Hodge and Phineas D. Gurley, I was assisted by an old friend, William O. Harris, who in the past twenty-five years has transformed the archives at the Robert E. Speer Library. At the Presbyterian Historical Society in Philadelphia, Ken Ross, a former student, helped me as I sought to learn more about Gurley.

My first readers have been my Huntington readers. My friend, Jack Rogers, philosopher and theologian, with whom I talked about Lincoln over countless lunches, read every chapter in various versions. Don Dewey brought not only his expertise in American history and politics but his editor's red pencil from his newspaper days to the entire manuscript. Charles Royster, whose book, *The Destructive War,* helped me think about Lincoln and war, read the first five chapters while in residence at the Huntington. Finally, Paul Zall, who knows more than anyone about Lincoln's wit, constantly cheered me on as I worked to appreciate Lincoln's wisdom.

Jim McPherson encouraged this project from the beginning and read every word. Jim, who was my teacher at Princeton University, served as the R. Stanton Avery Distinguished Fellow at the Huntington in 1994–95, the year the idea for what was then a single chapter on Lincoln's Second Inaugural was being born. Whether at the Huntington, or in visits to Princeton, or during conversations at changeovers on the tennis courts at Flint Canyon, the Atheneum, or Princeton University, I have benefited from the depth of Jim's enormous learning and artistic writing on Lincoln and the Civil War.

Many others have been kind enough to read portions of this book. Mark Noll, in the midst of a prodigious writing schedule, helped me think about Lincoln, Old and New School Presbyterians, and providence. Douglass Strong, an expert in antislavery politics and theology, read several chapters in an earlier version. Dr. Elaine Morrison Foster, a member of the New York Avenue Presbyterian Church and a researcher at the Library of Congress, shared with me resources about Phineas Densmore Gurley, New York Avenue Church, and Presbyterians in Washington in the nineteenth century.

The ideas that would help form this book first came into being as part of three seminars on Lincoln offered in the history department at UCLA. I am grateful to the UCLA students who were willing to go with me both to the Huntington and the Lincoln Shrine in Redlands as we all sought to go deeper into Lincoln. My colleague in the history department, Scott S. Bartchy, invited me to make a presentation on Lincoln to the interdepartmental colloquial of the Center for the Study of Religion.

My faculty colleagues at San Francisco Theological Seminary offered me their wise counsel in the presentation of chapter four in our faculty colloquia. Shelley Calkins, the Coordinator of Faculty Services, helped me with numerous tasks. I thank the faculty, Presidents Donald W. McCullough and James G. Emerson and the board of trustees, for granting me the sabbatical during which the bulk of the writing took place and for their continuing support.

The History Area of the Graduate Theological Union at Berkeley provided helpful responses in a presentation of chapter three.

I want to thank three able research assistants. Lee Hayden, who earned Phi Beta Kappa honors at UCLA, was indefatigable in his interest and help at the very beginning. Margo Houts helped find and read the old newspapers that became the backbone of chapter nine. Finally, Annie Russell, a Ph.D. student, is research assistant extraordinaire. Annie checked and formatted the endnotes, but more than that, she has become a partner in conversation about the shape of the book.

I wish to acknowledge that the seedbed of this book was a chapter written for *Religion and the American Civil War*, published by Oxford University Press in 1998. I thank the editors, Randall M. Miller, Harry S. Stout, and Charles Reagan Wilson, for their affirmation of my essay. Randall M. Miller was an especially helpful editor of my essay. Mark E. Neeley Jr., while in residence at the Huntington, read that chapter and helped me appreciate the political points of view of nineteenth-century newspapers.

All through this project I have been grateful to Petey Thornton, my secretary at San Francisco Theological Seminary. Her interest and help in this project was enthusiastic as always.

Sidney D. Kirkpatrick, a marvelous writer, encouraged me and opened a door to help make this book possible.

A special thanks to John and Lois Harrison. John, a gifted film writer and director, helped me think cinematically about placing the reader at the dramatic events of March 4, 1865. Lois generously hosted a gathering of friends to mark the transition of Lincoln's Second Inaugural from proposal to publishing project.

My literary agent, Mary Evans, has been a champion of this project from the beginning. Mary helped me learn and unlearn in a new venture. Mary knows how to affirm and critique with wit and energy.

I want to thank my growing number of friends at Simon & Schuster. Associate editor, Anja Schmidt, has helped shepherd this project from day one. Victoria Meyer and Rebecca Davis have been ready in every way to assist with publicity. Isolde C. Sauer has been in charge of copy editing. A special thanks to copy editor Anne T. Zaroff-Evans.

For me everything at Simon & Schuster begins and ends with Alice Mayhew. Her belief in the project buoyed my spirits along the way. Alice may say she is offering "just a little tightening," but I have benefited immeasurably from the wealth of her insight about the craft of writing. The whole project has been so delightful because of the privilege of working with Alice Mayhew.

Finally, I want to thank my wife, Cynthia, an associate dean at the University of Southern California. She is a marvelous photographer, and the credit for the author photograph on the jacket is hers. She is a thoughtful reader who offered her insights at each step of this project. She has been both encouraging and patient, as I would emerge from the world of the Civil War and the nineteenth century to regale her with Lincoln and the Second Inaugural Address.

INDEX

PHOTOGRAPHY CREDITS

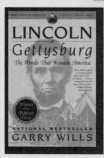

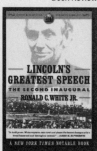
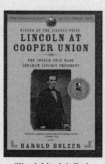